CHASING GOD
WITH THREE
FLAT TIRES

REALLIFE**STUFF**FOR**MEN** ON FAITH

A BIBLE DISCUSSION GUIDE FEATURING

NAVPRESS®

BRINGING TRUTH TO LIFE

OUR GUARANTEE TO YOU

We believe so strongly in the message of our books that we are making this quality guarantee to you. If for any reason you are disappointed with the content of this book, return the title page to us with your name and address and we will refund to you the list price of the book. To help us serve you better, please briefly describe why you were disappointed. Mail your refund request to: NavPress, P.O. Box 35002, Colorado Springs, CO 80935.

The Navigators is an international Christian organization. Our mission is to reach, disciple, and equip people to know Christ and to make Him known through successive generations. We envision multitudes of diverse people in the United States and every other nation who have a passionate love for Christ, live a lifestyle of sharing Christ's love, and multiply spiritual laborers among those without Christ.

NavPress is the publishing ministry of The Navigators. NavPress publications help believers learn biblical truth and apply what they learn to their lives and ministries. Our mission is to stimulate spiritual formation among our readers.

ISBN 1-57683-820-X

Cover design by Arvid Wallen
Cover illustration by Jared Lee
Creative Team: Steve Parolini, Cara Iverson, Pat Reinheimer

Written and compiled by Tim McLaughlin

Some of the anecdotal illustrations in this book are true to life and are included with the permission of the persons involved. All other illustrations are composites of real situations, and any resemblance to people living or dead is coincidental.

All Scripture quotations in this publication are taken from *THE MESSAGE* (MSG). Copyright © 1993, 1994, 1995, 1996, 2000, 2001, 2002. Used by permission of NavPress Publishing Group.

Printed in Canada

1 2 3 4 5 6 7 8 9 10 / 09 08 07 06 05

FOR A FREE CATALOG OF NAVPRESS BOOKS & BIBLE STUDIES,
CALL 1-800-366-7788 (USA) OR 1-800-839-4769 (CANADA)

CONTENTS

ABOUT THE
REALLIFESTUFFFORMEN
SERIES

Let your love dictate how you deal with me;
  teach me from your textbook on life.
I'm your servant — help me understand what that means,
  the inner meaning of your instructions. . . .
Break open your words, let the light shine out,
  let ordinary people see the meaning.

—PSALM 119:124-125,130

We're all yearning for understanding—for truth, wisdom, and hope. Whether we suffer in the simmering quiet of uncertainty or the megaphone cacophony of disbelief, we long for a better life—a more meaningful existence. We want to be Men Who Matter. But the fog of "real life stuff" we encounter every day obscures the life we crave, so we go on with the way things are.

Sometimes we pretend we don't care.

We do.

Sometimes we pretend everything is fine.

It isn't.

The truth is, the real life stuff matters. In that fog, there are things about our wives, our children, our friends, our work, and, most significantly, ourselves that cause varying degrees of distress, discomfort, and dis-ease.

The REAL LIFE STUFF FOR MEN series is a safe place for exploring the truth about that fog. But it's not a typical Bible study. You won't find any fill-in-the-blank questions in these pages. Nor will you find any pat answers. It's likely you'll come away with more questions rather than fewer. But through personal reflection and—in a small group—lively discussion (the best part of a Bible study anyway), these books will take you where you *need* to go and bring greater hope and meaning to your life.

Each of the books in this series provides a place to ask the hard questions of yourself and others, a place to find comfort in the chaos, a place to enlarge understanding, and—with the guidance of the Holy Spirit—a place to discover Real Life Hope that brings meaning to the everyday.

INTRODUCTION

Anything worth having is worth working for. So said your grandmother (or father or Little League coach or biology teacher), and you've found some truth in this. You set your eyes on a woman or a job or a car or some other goal, and then you started working, sweating, pursuing. And as often as not, you chased down what you wanted.

Jesus is said to be standing at the door knocking, but many men feel as though they're out beating the brush for him, tracking him, and following up on clues. Any Christ sightings are secondhand, told to you by glassy-eyed or just plain grateful Christians who testify to an enviable intimacy with Christ. If only that'd happen to you.

Yet on you go, clunking or cruising through life, through your career (probably more than one), through your marriage, trying all the time to chase down God, to grab him for your own like Jacob clutched the angel as if it were life itself (see Genesis 32:24-26). Even after that midnight bout, Jacob pursued God, gimpy leg notwithstanding. And as you pursue God with your own physical or emotional or spiritual disabilities, and even when you go months or even years without a scent of him, God still expects you to stay strong in faith, to abide in him—which is one reason Christ gave us the church. He wanted to give us camaraderie and encouragement, to at least give us each other when Christ sightings are few and far between.

But what happens when church loses its luster? When worship becomes irrelevant? When you wonder why your church became so bottom-line-driven?

Between Sundays, your private faith may waver more than you admit *on* Sundays. Your daily Bible-and-prayer time may have dried up years ago, or maybe you're still plowing ahead with it but without the return on your investment that you experienced early in your spiritual journey.

This is what we'll be exploring in *Chasing God with Three Flat Tires*. How do you cope with a faith that seems to have changed its shape or flavor or feeling? What does your uncertainty or the current tepidity of your faith say about you? About God? And how can you get back that lovin' feeling for God and his work? Is such a return impossible, or should you just limp along on your flat tires into something else? And what if that something else is really, really different from what you're used to, what you've been prepared for, what you've pictured as "spiritual maturity"?

Welcome to the mystery, which requires equal amounts of faith and sweat. If you didn't get it when your grandmother said as much, get it now from Paul:

> God's wisdom is something mysterious that goes deep
> into the interior of his purposes. You don't find it lying
> around on the surface. It's not the latest message, but
> more like the oldest—what God determined as the
> way to bring out his best in us, long before we ever
> arrived on the scene. The experts of our day haven't a
> clue about what this eternal plan is. If they had, they
> wouldn't have killed the Master of the God-designed life
> on a cross. That's why we have this Scripture text:
>
>> No one's ever seen or heard anything like this,
>> Never so much as imagined anything quite like it—
>> What God has arranged for those who love him.
>
> —1 CORINTHIANS 2:7-9

Maybe it's time to stop trying to chase down Jesus with only one or two good tires. Maybe you should pull off the road and get out of the car, because Jesus may not be on the road at all. Maybe with the engine off you can hear better, too. Maybe, just for a season, what you really need is less chasing and more listening.

HOW TO USE THIS DISCUSSION GUIDE

This discussion guide is meant to be completed on your own and in a small group. So before you begin, line up a discussion group. Perhaps you already participate in a men's group. That works. Maybe you know a few friends who could do coffee once a week. That works, too. Ask around. You'll be surprised how many of your coworkers, team members, and neighbors would be interested in a small-group study—especially a study like this that doesn't require vast biblical knowledge. A group of four to six is optimal—any bigger and one or more members will likely be shut out of discussions. Your small group can also be two. Choose a friend who isn't afraid to "tell it like it is." Make sure each person has his own copy of the book.

1. *Read* the Scripture passages and other readings in each lesson on your own. Let it all soak in. Then use the white space provided to "think out loud on paper." Note content in the readings that troubles you, inspires you, confuses you, or challenges you. Be honest. Be bold. Don't shy away from the hard things. If you don't understand the passage, say so. If you don't agree, say that, too. You may choose to go over the material in one thirty- to forty-five-minute focused session. Or perhaps you'll spend twenty minutes a day on the readings.

2. *Think* about what you read. Think about what you wrote. Always ask, "What does this mean?" and "Why does this matter?" about

the readings. Compare different Bible translations. Respond to the questions we've provided. You may have a lot to say on one topic, little on another. That's okay. Come back to this when you're in your small group. Allow the experience of others to broaden your wisdom. You'll be stretched here—called upon to evaluate what you've discovered and asked to make practical sense of it. In community, that stretching can often be painful and sometimes even embarrassing. But your willingness to be transparent—your openness to the possibility of personal growth—will reap great rewards.

3. *Pray* as you go through the entire session: before you read a word, in the middle of your thinking process, when you get stuck on a concept or passage, and as you approach the time when you'll explore these passages and thoughts together in a small group. Pause when you need to ask God for inspiration or when you need to cry out in frustration. Speak your prayers, be silent, or use the prayer starter we've provided and write a prayer at the end of each lesson.

4. *Live.* (That's "live" as in "rhymes with give" as in "Give me something I can really use in my life.") Before you meet with your small group, complete as much of this section as you can (particularly the "What I Want to Discuss" section). Then, in your small group, ask the hard questions about what the lesson means to you. Dig deep for relevant, reachable goals. Record your real-world plan in the book. Commit to following through on these plans, and prepare to be held accountable.

5. *Follow up.* Don't let the life application drift away without action. Be accountable to small-group members and refer to previous "Live" as in "rhymes with give" sections often. Take time at the beginning of each new study to review. See how you're doing.

6. *Repeat* as necessary.

SMALL-GROUP STUDY TIPS

After going through each week's study on your own, it's time to sit down with others and go deeper. Here are a few thoughts on how to make the most of your small-group discussion time.

Set ground rules. You don't need many. Here are two:

First, you'll want group members to make a commitment to the entire eight-week study. A binding legal document with notarized signatures and commitments written in blood probably isn't necessary, but you know your friends best. Just remember this: Significant personal growth happens when group members spend enough time together to really get to know each other. Hit-and-miss attendance rarely allows this to occur.

Second, agree together that everyone's story is important. Time is a valuable commodity, so if you have an hour to spend together, do your best to give each person ample time to express concerns, pass along insights, and generally feel like a participating member of the group. Small-group discussions are not monologues. However, a one-person-dominated discussion isn't always a bad thing. Not only is your role in a small group to explore and expand your own understanding, it's also to support one another. If someone truly needs more of the floor, give it to him. There will be times when the needs of the one outweigh the needs of the many. Use good judgment and allow extra space when needed. *Your* time might be next week.

Meet regularly. Choose a time and place, and stick to it. No one likes showing up to Coffee Cupboard at 6:00 AM, only to discover the meeting was moved to Breakfast Barn at seven. Consistency removes stress that could otherwise frustrate discussion and subsequent personal growth. It's only eight weeks. You can do this.

Talk openly. If you enter this study with shields up, you're probably not alone. And you're not a "bad person" for your hesitation to unpack your life in front of friends or strangers. Maybe you're skeptical about the value of revealing the deepest parts of who you are to others. Maybe you're simply too afraid of what might fall out of the suitcase. You don't have to go to a place where you're uncomfortable. If you want to sit and listen, offer a few thoughts, or even express a surface level of your own pain, go ahead. But don't neglect what brings you to this place — that longing for meaning. You can't ignore it away. Dip your feet in the water of brutally honest discussion, and you may choose to dive in. There is healing here.

Stay on task. Refrain from sharing material that falls into the "too much information" category. Don't spill unnecessary stuff, such as your wife's penchant for midnight bedroom belly dancing or your boss's obsession with Jennifer Aniston. This is about discovering how you can be a better person.

If structure isn't your group's strength, try a few minutes of general comments about the study, and then take each "Live" question one at a time and give everyone in the group a chance to respond. That should get you into the meat of matters pretty quickly.

Hold each other accountable. That "Live" section is an important gear in the growth machine. If you're really ready for positive change — for spiritual growth — you'll want to take this section seriously. Not only should you personally be thorough as you summarize your discoveries, practical as you compose your goals, and realistic as you determine the plan for accountability, you must hold everyone else in the group accountable for doing these things. Be lovingly, brutally honest as you examine each other's "Live" section. Don't hold back—this is where the rubber meets the road. A lack of openness here may send other group members skidding off that road.

CHURCH LEAVES ME COLD

*"I don't know if I'm just in a dry spell or
if my church is beating a dead horse."*

THE BEGINNING PLACE

It was in the mid-nineteenth century that the philosopher Søren
Kierkegaard drew this analogy in his *Purity of Heart Is to Will One
Thing*: A church typically considers its minister as the actor, God as the
prompter, and the congregation as the audience. To the contrary, wrote
the melancholy Dane: The congregation are the actors, the minister is
the prompter, and God is the audience.

If only, you think. If only you felt that a church service was actually
conducted for the benefit of God instead of to wow visitors and pacify
church members. If only you just once got the impression that the minister was directing the pastoral prayer to God instead of dressing up a
minisermon to look like a prayer. If only you could reconcile the sense
of Us versus Them you always leave church with: Christians versus
Non-Christians, Moral People versus Immoral People, Biblicists versus
Liberals, and so on. If only you could reconcile your church experience
with your experience of living and working among unchurched people
who need the gospel, but who you know wouldn't last ten minutes in
a sermon that made them the bad guys.

Maybe you'd give anything for a good old first-century judgment to fall on your church—a divine smiting a la Ananias and
Sapphira (see Acts 5). At least it would liven things up, get people's

attention—anything but the same old, same old that has character-ized that last five or ten years of your churchgoing experience. Or maybe you yearn to go to a church where you're a stranger; where you can slip into the back pew to be alone with your thoughts, alone with your God, alone with yourself; where you don't have to stand when told to stand; or where you can kneel for the entire service if you want to or slip out during the final hymn.

Maybe you're content with church—with worship—and wouldn't change much at all. What are your reasons for going to church? What factor in your Sunday morning, if it went missing, would tempt you to skip church? Friends? Sermons? Music? Ambiance? Child care? Socializing over coffee before or after services? Are there better and worse reasons to attend church? Or is any reason a good one that gets you there?

Or what are your reasons for not going to church? People? Sermons? Music? Ambiance? Child care? Weak coffee and no chocolate donuts?

Use the space below to summarize your beginning place for this lesson. Describe what church and worship does and doesn't do for you anymore and why you think that is. We'll start here and then go deeper.

READ A Proper Noun

From *Wishful Thinking*, by Frederick Buechner[1]

CHURCH. The visible church is all the people who get together from time to time in God's name. Anybody can find out who they are by going to church to look.

The invisible church is all the people God uses for his hands and feet in this world. Nobody can find out who they are except God.

Think of them as two circles. The optimist says they are concentric. The cynic says they don't even touch. The realist says they occasionally overlap.

In a fit of high inspiration, the author of the Book of Revelation states that there is no temple in the New Jerusalem, thus squelching once and for all the tedious quip that since Heaven is an endless church service, anybody with two wits to rub together would prefer Hell.

The reason for there being no temple in the New Jerusalem is presumably the same as the reason for Noah's leaving the ark behind when he finally makes it to Mount Ararat.

THINK

- Ponder Buechner's definition of "the invisible church." What do you agree with about it? What do you disagree with about it? Why?
- Right now in your experience with church, are the two circles Buechner describes concentric, overlapping, or not even touching each other?
- What circle or circles do you feel you've been in during the past few months or years?
- Do you feel at home in this circle, or do you have a nagging sense that you ought to be migrating in some direction or another? Think about this.

THINK (CONTINUED)

PRAY

God, challenge me . . .

READ She's Gonna Blow!

Matthew 16:15-18

He pressed them, "And how about you? Who do you say I am?"

Simon Peter said, "You're the Christ, the Messiah, the Son of the living God."

Jesus came back, "God bless you, Simon, son of Jonah! You didn't get that answer out of books or from teachers. My Father in heaven, God himself, let you in on this secret of who I really am. And now I'm going to tell you who you are, *really* are. You are Peter, a rock. This is the rock on which I will put together my church, a church so expansive with energy that not even the gates of hell will be able to keep it out."

THINK

- How does Jesus' description of his church compare with your current church experience?
- What do you suppose Jesus meant when he said that the gates of hell won't be able to keep his church out? In what sense was he speaking? Ideally? Realistically? Metaphorically?
- Describe a season or experience when church really was for you "expansive with energy."
- If church isn't this for you now, what one change would make it so?

THINK (CONTINUED)

PRAY

God, show me how . . .

READ Is It the Good Life or the Christ Life?

From *Inside Out*, by Larry Crabb[2]

Many of us have elements of the good life *plus* a Christian package of sincere commitment, moral integrity, and church involvement that helps us avoid the feeling that something is missing.

Is that style of life what Christ promised when He spoke of rivers of living water flowing through us? If we were honest, I suspect most of us would like to believe that personal comfort and spiritual commitment define the abundant life Jesus provides. . . . But the question must be asked: is that what springs of living water provide?

Many churches, particularly the ones that televise their services, make a habit of inviting only those whose lives are going well at the moment to share what Christ means to them. The message is consistent: comfort and commitment, both are available. Trust God to change whatever makes you uncomfortable while you choose to follow Him.

I have often wondered how much crippling guilt and soul-wracking pain those testimonies provoke in those who have committed themselves to Christ as best they can but whose lives are filled with terrible discomfort. As the speakers tell their stories of warm family reunions, children preparing for missionary service, relational tensions that have been replaced by joyful reconciliation, and financial losses that God has miraculously turned around, how many hearts rejoice in God's goodness? . . .

Those folks whose struggles are more pressing—broken marriages, rebellious kids, aching loneliness—well, we can only pray that God will restore their personal comforts as they continue to trust Him.

This kind of response turns church into a country club offering its benefits to those who are fortunate enough and well-mannered enough to qualify for membership. We sit Sunday after Sunday enjoying the fellowship of others who are comfortable and committed while the brokenhearted and poor press their noses against the window, looking in at us with resentment, envy, and despair.

THINK

- How comfortable are you and other church members with visitors of an obviously different socioeconomic level? What makes you feel the way you do?
- Respond to this generalization: "People in poor churches thank God for the blessing of spiritual wealth; people in affluent churches thank God for the blessing of affluence." How does your church connect financial status with spirituality?
- When was the last time you heard a glowing testimony, such as what Crabb describes, and felt absolutely miserable? Why the misery?
- If you had anything to say about it, how would a church rejoice with the joyful without making those who had nothing to rejoice about feel guilty?

PRAY

God, open the door . . .

READ Woohoo! Worship!

Psalm 100

On your feet now—applaud GOD!
Bring a gift of laughter,
sing yourselves into his presence.

Know this: GOD is God, and God, GOD.
He made us; we didn't make him.
We're his people, his well-tended sheep.

Enter with the password: "Thank you!"
Make yourselves at home, talking praise.
Thank him. Worship him.

For GOD is sheer beauty,
all-generous in love,
loyal always and ever.

THINK

- Compare your churchgoing experience with that described in this psalm. What are the similarities? Differences?
- In this brief but ecstatic psalm, list the commands (for example, "*Bring* a gift of laughter"). How might these benefit your church-going experience?
- According to this psalmist, what is the reward for our worship of God?
- What would it take to make you feel like this psalmist about worship?

THINK (CONTINUED)

PRAY

Lord, help me to feel at home . . .

READ I Will *Never* Do That

From Annie Dillard (in *The Sun*)[3]

He had vowed long ago, and renewed his vow frequently, that if holding hands in a circle and singing hymns . . . was what it took to make life endurable, he would rather die.

From *Experiential Worship*, by Bob Rognlien[4]

If we are committed to helping people experience God today, we will go far beyond the latest techniques to the core of what worship is really about. We will learn whole new languages. Like those brave cross-cultural missionaries who have gone before us, we will become ongoing students of emerging cultures, continually interpreting and explaining the context of our particular ministries. We will rediscover the arts as a means of conveying the infinite to the finite and unleash artists to share their gifts with the community. We will seek to understand personality types and learning styles and the impact of different modes of communication. We will utilize the latest technology as the vernacular of our time. We will learn from the whole spectrum of Christian tradition in order to renew and invigorate our own stream of the faith. We will break out of our comfort zones and explore all God has for us on what Brian McLaren calls "the other side" of this postmodern cultural revolution.

THINK

- List a few things that absolutely drive you crazy—or drive you away—when you encounter them in church services.
- How does the charge to pastors in the *Experiential Worship* excerpt match with your actual experience of church?
- How can churches accomplish the goal of helping to "make life endurable" in the way they approach the worship service? Where do you find this in your experience, if at all?

- When you recognize how much you dislike something about a church service, do you tend to beat yourself up about it, or do you blow it off? Is it a real problem in the church, or is it just *your* spiritual problem?

PRAY

Lord, teach me to worship . . .

READ The Run of the House

Colossians 3:16

> Let the Word of Christ—the Message—have the run of the
> house. Give it plenty of room in your lives. Instruct and direct
> one another using good common sense. And sing, sing your
> hearts out to God!

THINK

- On a scale of one to ten, how much do you feel your church
  lets "the Word of Christ—the Message—have the run of the
  house"?
- What would a higher score look like at your church?
- On a scale of one to ten, how much do you feel your church
  uses "good common sense"? What would a higher score in *this*
  category look like?
- In your experience, how well are churches doing today with
  the singing exhortation that Paul gives first-century Christians?
- Do you feel music has become too important to modern
  churchgoers, or do you feel that music is not given its rightful
  place in most worship services?

PRAY

God, lead me to find . . .

LIVE

What I Want to Discuss

What have you discovered this week that you definitely want to discuss with your small group? Write that here. Then begin your small-group discussion with these thoughts.

So What?

Use the following space to summarize what you've discovered about your disappointment with church and worship. Review your "Beginning Place" if you need to remember where you began. How does God's truth impact the "next step" in your journey?

Then What?

What is one practical thing you can do to apply what you've discovered? Describe how you would put this into practice. What steps would you take? Remember to think realistically—an admirable but unreachable goal is as good as no goal. Discuss your goal in your small group to further define it.

How?

Identify how you will be held accountable to the goal you described. Who will be on your support team? What are their responsibilities? How will you measure the success of your plan? Write the details here.

WHAT QUIET TIME?

"Why does the idea of daily devotions give me
guilt rather than inspiration?"

A REMINDER:

Before you dive into this study, spend a little time reviewing what you wrote in the previous lesson's "Live" sections. How are you doing? Check with your small-group members and review your progress toward the specified goals. If necessary, adjust your goals and plans, and then recommit to them.

THE BEGINNING PLACE

Why do you—or why should you—read your Bible and pray?

The answers you hear—at church, in Christian books, and via broadcasts—is that the Bible is the Word of God. There is no truth apart from the Bible. There is no truth higher than the Bible. The Bible contains all you need. The Bible will keep you from sin, keep you humble, keep you productive for the kingdom, keep you living like a Christian. The Bible will even make you a shrewd manager of money, an effective raiser of children, a passionate spouse.

With promises like these, who wouldn't read his Bible ravenously?

And then there's prayer—communicating with God, confessing your sins, confiding your secrets. "Pray all the time," Paul urges the ancient Christians of Thessalonica (1 Thessalonians 5:17), and your pastor or Bible study teacher passes along this apostolic instruction to you.

It is at this juncture that your Bible, your prayers, and often a smidgen (or more) of uncertainty meet. How exactly do you "pray all the time"? If you prayed all the time, nothing else in your day would get done! Perhaps Paul meant it metaphorically: He used a figure of speech or exaggerated his point for emphasis. Yet if you interpret this four-word verse figuratively, where do you stop? What happens to the literal interpretation of the Bible?

Your answers to such questions, of course, determine how you read the Bible, how you pray, and what you expect from those two spiritual activities. What many pastors and Sunday school teachers and Christian camp counselors and Christian writers suggest is a daily, systematic, and personal reading of the Bible and saying of prayers—preferably first thing in the morning. This ritual is known as one's "quiet time" or "personal devotions" or "getting alone with God" or being "in the Word" or being a "prayer warrior."

So how's your "quiet time"? Heard from God lately? If so, what? If not, why not? Do your personal devotions fuel you for the day, or have you stopped making the attempt? And is guilt now nagging you for ignoring God's Word?

Use the space below to summarize your beginning place for this lesson. Describe your "quiet time" disasters and successes, your current love affair or disenchantment (or wherever in the middle you may fall) with daily devotions, and what you wish your devotional life could look like. We'll start here and then go deeper.

READ Pray It Like Jesus

Matthew 6:5-15

"When you come before God, don't turn that into a theatrical production. . . . All these people making a regular show out of their prayers, hoping for stardom! Do you think God sits in a box seat?

"Here's what I want you to do: Find a quiet, secluded place so you won't be tempted to role-play before God. Just be there as simply and honestly as you can manage. The focus will shift from you to God, and you will begin to sense his grace.

"The world is full of so-called prayer warriors who are prayer-ignorant. They're full of formulas and programs and advice, peddling techniques for getting what you want from God. Don't fall for that nonsense. This is your Father you are dealing with, and he knows better than you what you need. With a God like this loving you, you can pray very simply. Like this:

> Our Father in heaven,
> Reveal who you are.
> Set the world right;
> Do what's best—
>   as above, so below.
> Keep us alive with three square meals.
> Keep us forgiven with you and forgiving others.
> Keep us safe from ourselves and the Devil.
> You're in charge!
> You can do anything you want!
> You're ablaze in beauty!
>   Yes. Yes. Yes.

"In prayer there is a connection between what God does and what you do. You can't get forgiveness from God, for instance, without also forgiving others. If you refuse to do your part, you cut yourself off from God's part."

THINK

- What formulas, programs, advice, or techniques for devotional praying have you tried? Have any of them worked for you?
- What role-playing have you noticed yourself doing as you pray?
- "Keep us alive . . ." "Keep us forgiven . . ." "Keep us safe from ourselves . . ." How would you feel if your minister prayed this way publicly next Sunday morning?
- Describe the circumstances around a time when you've felt a very close connection with God during prayer.

PRAY

God, teach me to pray . . .

READ Keep It Simple

From *Two-Part Invention*, by Madeleine L'Engle[1]

Ellis Peters, in *A Morbid Taste for Bones*, one of her delight-
ful medieval whodunits, gives a beautiful description of what I
believe to be intercessory prayer: "He prayed as he breathed,
forming no words and making no specific requests, only holding
in his heart, like broken birds in cupped hands, all those people
who were in stress or grief."

From "The Sayings of the Fathers," in *Seeking a Purer Spiritual Life*[2]

Abba Macarius was asked, "How should one pray?" The old
man said, "There is no need at all to make long discourses; it is
enough to stretch out one's hands and say, 'Lord, as you will,
and as you know, have mercy.' And if the conflict grows fiercer,
say, 'Lord, help!' God knows very well what we need and shows
us mercy."

THINK

- What are your first reactions to these words? Do they seem
  simplistic to you? Profoundly true? Unlike you've ever prayed
  before? Just like you've prayed before?
- Have you ever prayed for someone "forming no words and
  making no specific requests"? What was that like?
- How do you reconcile these two apparent truths: God knows
  better than you what you need, and God wants you to pray for
  it anyway.
- If regular prayer is difficult for you to do, why? If it's easy for
  you, why?

THINK (CONTINUED)

PRAY

Lord, hear my prayers . . .

READ Holy Bore

From *Wishful Thinking*, by Frederick Buechner[3]

One way to describe the Bible, written by many different people over a period of three thousand years and more, would be to say that it is a disorderly collection of sixty-odd books which are often tedious, barbaric, obscure, and teem with contradictions and inconsistencies. It is a swarming compost of a book, an Irish stew of poetry and propaganda, law and legalism, myth and murk, history and hysteria. Over the centuries it has become hopelessly associated with tub-thumping evangelism and dreary piety, with superannuated superstition and blue-nosed moralizing, with ecclesiastical authoritarianism and crippling literalism. Let them who try to start out at Genesis and work their way conscientiously to Revelation beware.

And yet just because it is a book about both the sublime and the unspeakable, it is a book also about life the way it really is. It is a book about people who at one and the same time can be both believing and unbelieving, innocent and guilty, crusaders and crooks, full of hope and full of despair. In other words, it is a book about us.

And it is also a book about God. If it is not about the God we believe in, then it is about the God we do not believe in. One way or another, the story we find in the Bible is our own story. . . .

If you look *at* a window, you see flyspecks, dust, the crack where Junior's Frisbee hit it. If you look *through* a window, you see the world beyond.

Something like this is the difference between those who see the Bible as a Holy Bore and those who see it as the Word of God, which speaks out of the depths of an almost unimaginable past into the depths of ourselves.

THINK

- What are your earliest memories of reading the Bible?
- Which of Buechner's characterizations of the Bible do you identify with most?
- Have you generally grown up with your current view of the Bible, or has it become a different book to you now than it once was? If the latter, what triggered the change?
- At its core, is the Bible a book about God, or is it a book about us? Why do you think that?

PRAY

Lord, illuminate your Word . . .

READ Tie Them on Your Hands

Deuteronomy 6:6-9

> Write these commandments that I've given you today on your
> hearts. Get them inside of you and then get them inside your
> children. Talk about them wherever you are, sitting at home or
> walking in the street; talk about them from the time you get up
> in the morning to when you fall into bed at night. Tie them on
> your hands and foreheads as a reminder; inscribe them on the
> doorposts of your homes and on your city gates.

THINK

- What do you think God is speaking about in this passage?
- What implications does this passage have about how to spend
  your time with God?
- In your experience, is a person who lives with such intense
  connection to God's Word more able or less able to connect
  with mundane, day-to-day life around him?
- What are ways you could live out the spirit of these verses,
  whether or not you "tie them on your hands and forehead"?

PRAY

God, draw me to you . . .

READ How to Read the Bible

From *Love Your God with All Your Mind*, by J. P. Moreland[4]

Certain steps are required in order to enter correctly into the process of devotional reading. First, you must get into a position of being ready to listen with the heart to the Holy Spirit as His quiet voice speaks to you about what you are reading. Before a devotional reading of *The Imitation of Christ* or prior to practicing *lectio divina* on a gospel text or a psalm (the four gospels, the Psalms, and the Wisdom Literature, especially Proverbs and Ecclesiastes, are the best texts for this type of reading), sit quietly, confess any sin that comes to mind (and promise to make reconciliation if that is needed), and express tender devotion to God with whatever sincerity you can muster at this stage of the process. Then invite God to speak to your heart about what you are reading.

Second, with a spirit of expectancy and an attitude of openness and vulnerability, read the selected text slowly, calmly, and with an open, vulnerable heart. The goal here is not to read a lot of material, but to enter into a small portion of a book or of the Scripture. While reading, seek to monitor what is happening inside your own soul. Do not try to master the passage, but allow the passage to master you. Third, throughout the process of reading, you may sense the need to stop, to meditate and contemplate a specific meaning in the text, and to enter into a dialogue with God about that meaning.

Finally, it is important to recognize that this type of slow, contemplative reading will frequently be met with hindrances that distract or discourage you. Especially discouraging is the sense that the text is not as moving as you had hoped. The proper response when this happens is to stop reading, allow yourself to feel whatever is going on inside, offer the situation to God, and rededicate yourself to continuing to learn how to get better at this type of reading. With practice and persevering dedication, you will benefit deeply from such contemplative openness before God.

THINK

- What do you think of Moreland's steps to reading the Bible devotionally?
- How can you "enter into a dialogue with God" about the meaning of a Bible text?
- How might this kind of contemplative reading affect your devotional life?
- Do you appreciate or require structure in your devotional life? Do spiritual checklists help focus you, or do they distract you? Think about this.

PRAY

Father, help me to see your truth in Scripture . . .

READ The Freedom of a Regulated Life

From *Meditations: On the Monk Who Dwells in Daily Life*,
by Thomas Moore[5]

In a monastery time is carefully spent. Outside, we don't think much of letting one activity lead to another, each taking as much time as needed. But in a monastery there are fifteen minutes for reading, two hours for study, allotted periods for prayer and meditation, usually less than an hour here and there for recreation.

It does no good to think moralistically about how much time we waste. Wasted time is usually good soul time. But there is something especially fruitful in a regulated life, a fantasy of time in which regularity—monasticism is sometimes called the regular life—is not a prison but freedom.

The ritual quality of appointed times releases us from the burdens of free will.

THINK

• What do you think Moore means when he writes that "wasted time is usually good soul time"? Do you agree or disagree? Why?
• Does it seem contradictory or natural to you to speak of ritual and regulation being freedom, and free will being a burden?
• When in your experience has a regular and structured devotional time been a prison to you? What were the circumstances?
• When has a regular and structured devotional time been freedom for you? What did you feel freed from?

THINK (CONTINUED)

PRAY

Lord, show me the value of ritual . . .

LIVE

What I Want to Discuss

What have you discovered this week that you definitely want to discuss with your small group? Write that here. Then begin your small-group discussion with these thoughts.

So What?

Use the following space to summarize what you've discovered about your practice of personal devotion or "quiet time." Review your "Beginning Place" if you need to remember where you began. How does God's truth impact the "next step" in your journey?

Then What?

What is one practical thing you can do to apply what you've discovered? Describe how you would put this into practice. What steps would you take? Remember to think realistically—an admirable but unreachable goal is as good as no goal. Discuss your goal in your small group to further define it.

How?

Identify how you will be held accountable to the goal you described. Who will be on your support team? What are their responsibilities? How will you measure the success of your plan? Write the details here.

STEWARDSHIP
OF FOOLS?

"My church spiritualizes its use of money,
but isn't it all about the bottom line?"

A REMINDER:

Before you dive into this study, spend a little time reviewing what you wrote in the previous lesson's "Live" sections. How are you doing? Check with your small-group members and review your progress toward the specified goals. If necessary, adjust your goals and plans, and then recommit to them.

THE BEGINNING PLACE

The mix of money and faith has always simmered just a few degrees from flash point. While Moses was up the mountain, his brother persuaded the waiting and restless Israelites to lend some substance to this ethereal deity, Yahweh. So their gold became their god. Not much later, they again contributed gold to a religious purpose—this time to the furnishings of Yahweh's desert dwelling, the tabernacle.

When Solomon asked not for wealth or long life but for wisdom, God gave him wisdom—and wealth and long life. On the other hand, despite God's warning that Israel's kings shouldn't go around stockpiling military armament and money and wives, Solomon did just that. And it all turned around and bit him in the end.

During the Exile in Babylonia, many of the details of the Jewish law were spelled out and codified—including details about tithing, that 10 percent "tax" that God levied on his people. And so it came to pass that tithing became a public, visible gauge of one's devotion. The public part, however, quickly shoved aside the devotion part so that the Jews' Yahweh was soon castigating them for hypocrisy—for following the letter of the tithing law yet not getting its spiritual aspect.

The apostle Paul turned it all on its head when in the first century he wrote that the law no longer constrained Christians to giving 10 percent. Part of being freed from the law, he pointed out, was that Christians were also free to give more than 10 percent or less than 10 percent—whatever they decided to give—without feeling compelled, without grudging.

Since then, the Christian church has seesawed on the money-and-faith question. Popes levied taxes on the faithful in order to beautify cathedrals. Monks shunned money and embraced poverty to purify their souls. Like medieval priests and the indulgences they sold to the laity, modern televangelists are willing to grant spiritual healing if not forgiveness of sins to those who ante up a few bucks for a prayer hanky.

And then there's your church's annual Stewardship Sunday, when you get the money sermon and your pastor can't help but at least imply that God is pleased with you when you give money to your church and a bit irritated when you don't. You think, *If only they'd just come out and say it: "Like any nonprofit, this incorporated body needs regular donations if it is to exist. So step up to the plate, make your pledge, and make good on it!"* But no, they drag God into it, and it begins to smell of manipulation: "God will bless you if you give money—the more money, the more blessing."

Yet isn't there indeed a connection between your faith and your money? Hasn't one mark of Christians traditionally been how we take care of those who have less than we have, whether with food or clothing or cash? Or have you had bad experiences with church finances—fund-raising that went bad, or the wrong people entrusted with decision making?

Use the following space to summarize your beginning place for

READ Ah, Those Affluent Nontithers

From *The Discipline of Grace*, by Jerry Bridges[1]

I know that we get a lot of guilt laid on us in the United States about materialism, and I have no desire to lay guilt on someone just because he or she lives in a better house and eats better food than people in the less developed countries. But I recently heard a statistic that both alarmed and saddened me: Only 4 percent of evangelicals in the United States give a tithe (10 percent) of their income to God's work.

Even though some Christians question the applicability of the tithe concept in the New Testament era, this is still a shameful statistic. It means the overwhelming majority of professing Christians in the most affluent nation in history are spending most of their income on themselves.

On the other hand, those of us who do give 10 percent or more of our income to God's work can become proud and self-righteous about it as we look around and see others who are not as generous. In that case, all we are doing is exchanging one sin for another—the sin of materialism and selfishness for the sin of self-righteous pride.

THINK

- Do you believe God expects modern Christians to tithe—that is, give a minimum of 10 percent of one's income—no differently than he expected ancient Jews to? Why or why not?
- Is the meager proportion of U.S. evangelicals who tithe as shameful a statistic to you as it is to Bridges? Why or why not?
- If you were responsible for increasing your church's income, how would you do it? How would you avoid using guilt? (Or would you?) How would you avoid giving the impression that people who give more are more favored by God?

this lesson. Describe what you believe the Bible teaches about money, your experience with how your church collects and spends money and how you feel about it, and your own personal "stewardship history." We'll start here and then go deeper.

READ Put Me On the Payroll, Already!

1 Corinthians 9:3-12

I'm not shy in standing up to my critics. We who are on missionary assignments for God have a right to decent accommodations, and we have a right to support for us and our families. You don't seem to have raised questions with the other apostles and our Master's brothers and Peter in these matters. So, why me? Is it just Barnabas and I who have to go it alone and pay our own way? Are soldiers self-employed? Are gardeners forbidden to eat vegetables from their own gardens? Don't milkmaids get to drink their fill from the pail?

I'm not just sounding off because I'm irritated. This is all written in the scriptural law. Moses wrote, "Don't muzzle an ox to keep it from eating the grain when it's threshing." Do you think Moses' primary concern was the care of farm animals? Don't you think his concern extends to us? Of course. Farmers plow and thresh expecting something when the crop comes in. So if we have planted spiritual seed among you, is it out of line to expect a meal or two from you? Others demand plenty from you in these ways. Don't we who have never demanded deserve even more?

THINK

- What is your initial reaction to Paul's words?
- What would you think if a pastor or church staffer said this during a service, over coffee, or in your church newsletter?
- What are the unspoken rules in your church about money talk (when and when not to talk about it, acceptable and unacceptable words to use in talking about it, and so on)?
- Are the apostle's words here an airtight argument for how to deal with money today, or are there extenuating circumstances today that qualify Paul's argument?

THINK (CONTINUED)

PRAY

Lord, untangle these thoughts about money . . .

• What in your experience was the most appropriate approach a church took in obtaining an income that adequately funded its ministry (salaries, supplies, capital expenses, and so on)?

PRAY

God, help me see the truth about tithing . . .

READ Do What You Can, Not What You Can't

2 Corinthians 8:9-15; 9:6-11

You are familiar with the generosity of our Master, Jesus Christ.
Rich as he was, he gave it all away for us—in one stroke he
became poor and we became rich.

So here's what I think: The best thing you can do right now
is to finish what you started last year and not let those good
intentions grow stale. Your heart's been in the right place all
along. You've got what it takes to finish it up, so go to it. Once
the commitment is clear, you do what you can, not what you
can't. The heart regulates the hands. This isn't so others can take
it easy while you sweat it out. No, you're shoulder to shoulder
with them all the way, your surplus matching their deficit, their
surplus matching your deficit. In the end you come out even. As
it is written,

> Nothing left over to the one with the most,
> Nothing lacking to the one with the least. . . .

Remember: A stingy planter gets a stingy crop; a lavish
planter gets a lavish crop. I want each of you to take plenty of
time to think it over, and make up your own mind what you will
give. That will protect you against sob stories and arm-twisting.
God loves it when the giver delights in the giving.

God can pour on the blessings in astonishing ways so that
you're ready for anything and everything, more than just ready to
do what needs to be done. As one psalmist puts it,

> He throws caution to the winds,
>   giving to the needy in reckless abandon.
> His right-living, right-giving ways
>   never run out, never wear out.

This most generous God who gives seed to the farmer that becomes bread for your meals is more than extravagant with you. He gives you something you can then give away, which grows into full-formed lives, robust in God, wealthy in every way, so that you can be generous in every way, producing with us great praise to God.

THINK

- "Do what you can, not what you can't." How often have you heard *that* used as a principle for church giving? Is it valid? Why or why not?
- How easy or difficult is it for you to picture God throwing "caution to the winds" or acting "in reckless abandon"?
- What's the most recent instance of God being "more than extravagant with you"?
- What did the apostle write was the reason God was generous with his children? Think about this.

PRAY

Father, pour on your blessings . . .

READ Church Finances of the Third Century

**From Tertullian in *Selections from Early Christian Writers*,
by Henry Melvill Gwatkin[2]**

Our presidents are the approved elders, obtaining that honour
not for a price, but by attested character; for indeed the things of
God are not sold for a price. Even if there is a sort of common
fund, it is not made up of money paid in fees, as for a worship
by contract. Each of us puts in a trifle on the monthly day, or
when he pleases; but only if he pleases, and only if he is able,
for no man is obliged, but contributes of his own free will. These
are as it were deposits of piety; for it is not paid out thence for
feasts and drinkings and thankless eating-houses, but for feeding
and burying the needy, for boys and girls deprived of means and
parents, for old folk now confined to the house: also for them
that are shipwrecked, for any who are in the mines, and for any
who are in the islands or in the prisons.

THINK

- According to this third-century "explainer" of Christian ways to
a pagan world, how did the early church collect money? How
did the early church *spend* money?
- What might the modern equivalents be of ancient shipwrecks,
mines, islands of exile, and the wants of "boys and girls
deprived of means and parents"?
- How does your church compare to Tertullian's description of
how the early church collected and spent money? Is such a
comparison fair to attempt? Why or why not?

THINK (CONTINUED)

PRAY

Lord, teach me how to contribute . . .

READ The Forest or the Trees?

Matthew 23:23-24

"You're hopeless, you religion scholars and Pharisees! Frauds! You keep meticulous account books, tithing on every nickel and dime you get, but on the meat of God's Law, things like fairness and compassion and commitment—the absolute basics!—you carelessly take it or leave it. Careful bookkeeping is commendable, but the basics are required. Do you have any idea how silly you look, writing a life story that's wrong from start to finish, nitpicking over commas and semicolons?"

From *Fed Up*, by 30 Hour Famine with Tim McLaughlin[3]

A Very, Very Brief History of Jewish and Christian Belief:

- When the Law came down the slopes of Mt. Sinai cradled in Moses' arms, belief was, as they say, codified. God's words were now engraved in stone (if not in black and white . . . that would come later, when ink was applied to parchment). There was no guessing, no wondering if you heard God clearly in your head or your heart. You say you loved Yahweh? Put your sacrificial doves where your mouth is and prove it—by obeying the letter of the law. Of course, it was hoped that one observed the feast days and sacrificed their best fruits and livestock and kept their eyes from wandering to their neighbors' wives because, at the bottom of it all, they actually *loved* Yahweh and believed that keeping the Law was in their best interest. But you know how laws are easy to keep even when you don't believe in them. Laws are *especially* easy to keep when you don't believe in them but want to give others the impression that you *do*.
- Jesus upset the apple cart (and the dove cages and the money tables in the temple) when he reminded his country's

religious leaders that if they all kept the letter of the Law but not its spirit, they were missing the point—which, it so happened, was exactly and unfortunately the case. Jesus wouldn't let this rest, either, but kept hammering these religious leaders at every opportunity for (among other things) not taking care of people in the lower strata of society—the poor, the lepers, the widows, the whores, the maimed. Read it for yourself in Matthew 23:23-24, when Jesus lowered the boom on the religious leaders for nitpicking their way through figuring out exactly what they owed God to the penny but meanwhile ignored issues of justice and mercy.

THINK

- How likely is it that your pastor could get away with talking to your congregation like Jesus talked to his audience in the Matthew passage?
- Have churches in your experience considered tithing (or giving or stewardship) among "the absolute basics"? If so, how do such beliefs compare with these words of Jesus?
- What parts of a church's "life story" does it typically overlook while it stresses stewardship, giving, or tithing?
- What proportion of your church's income goes to "taking care of people in the lower strata of society"? Who in your community *are* the lower strata of society?

THINK (CONTINUED)

PRAY

God, help my church to discover . . .

READ The Nobility of Begging

From *Meditations: On the Monk Who Dwells in Daily Life*,
by Thomas Moore[4]

My community was called a mendicant order—begging living off alms. Today begging is shameful to the middle class, a scandal to those who think everyone can and should work for a living. The homeless person on the street is surrounded by the emotional shadows of reprobation.

Yet, the most spiritual activities are funded by begging: public radio and television, charities, programs for the disadvantaged, medicine, education. Even today many who enter the most meaningful professions become mendicants.

If we are not beggars, we might ask ourselves if we have any spirituality in our lives.

THINK

- Do you agree with Moore that begging is shameful and a scandal to the middle class? Why or why not?
- How accurate do you feel Moore's analogy is of begging to the funding of nonprofit organizations?
- Would you characterize how your church solicits funds as *begging*? If not, what word *would* describe it?
- In what ways might your spirituality increase if you became a beggar, at least in some sense?

THINK (CONTINUED)

PRAY

God, grant me humility . . .

LIVE

What I Want to Discuss

What have you discovered this week that you definitely want to discuss with your small group? Write that here. Then begin your small-group discussion with these thoughts.

So What?

Use the following space to summarize what you've discovered about your spiritual inertia, along with any hopes or ways to get your faith in gear again. Review your "Beginning Place" if you need to remember where you began. How does God's truth impact the "next step" in your journey?

Then What?

What is one practical thing you can do to apply what you've discovered? Describe how you would put this into practice. What steps would you take? Remember to think realistically—an admirable but unreachable goal is as good as no goal. Discuss your goal in your small group to further define it.

How?

Identify how you will be held accountable to the goal you described. Who will be on your support team? What are their responsibilities? How will you measure the success of your plan? Write the details here.

SO, HOW LONG WILL GOD BE ON VACATION?

"I'm running out of explanations for God's silence when I need answers most."

A REMINDER:

Before you dive into this study, spend a little time reviewing what you wrote in the previous lesson's "Live" sections. How are you doing? Check with your small-group members and review your progress toward the specified goals. If necessary, adjust your goals and plans, and then recommit to them.

THE BEGINNING PLACE

If you've grown up in the church, you know firsthand how the doctrine of God's silence has gotten short shrift.

In Fours and Fives Sunday school, you heard—and saw illustrated with flannelgraph—that God hears and answers the prayers of a little child.

A decade later in youth group you were taught that however brutal high school was for you socially, God was your best friend, always at your side, always eager to listen to you when you trusted no one else with your adolescent anxieties.

As an adult you are taught the three "omnis" of God's nature— omniscient, omnipotent, omnipresent, with accompanying biblical proofs. God is all-knowledgeable, all-powerful, and all-present.

Notice something God is *not*: Like a good friend, he is not all-talkable. He's always there but not always speaking—which is the nice way to say it. The dark side is when you desperately want—*need*—to hear him but don't; when you follow all the appropriate Christian incantations to get a comforting or directive word from God but hear nothing; when you plead, cajole, beg, go forward in church, speak in tongues, offer yourself, offer your firstborn—*anything* for some indication that the Almighty is listening, that he cares, that he's doing anything for you in your duress. And for your trouble, only silence.

So where was the sermon series on "The Silence of God"? After Mrs. Meersma gave her glowing testimony of how God answered her prayer—in fact, spoke to her *almost every morning* during her "quiet time" with the Lord—why wasn't Don Wilkens called up front to give *his* testimony about how he's been asking God for relief and guidance in a domestic horror story but things have only gotten worse. And as far as Don can tell, God has withdrawn from the situation even further than Don's wife has withdrawn from him.

So how silent or how talkative is God these days with you? Has God recently broken a long silence? How did you do during his "absence"? *What* did you do during it? Did you try to figure out a reason for the silence?

Use the space below to summarize your beginning place for this lesson. Describe what you have experienced from or heard about the silence of God. Also explain how you coped or are coping. We'll start here and then go deeper.

READ Abandoned by God

Mark 15:25-37

They nailed him up at nine o'clock in the morning. The charge against him—THE KING OF THE JEWS—was printed on a poster. Along with him, they crucified two criminals, one to his right, the other to his left. People passing along the road jeered, shaking their heads in mock lament: "You bragged that you could tear down the Temple and then rebuild it in three days—so show us your stuff! Save yourself! If you're really God's Son, come down from that cross!"

The high priests, along with the religion scholars, were right there mixing it up with the rest of them, having a great time poking fun at him: "He saved others—but he can't save himself! Messiah, is he? King of Israel? Then let him climb down from that cross. We'll *all* become believers then!" Even the men crucified alongside him joined in the mockery.

At noon the sky became extremely dark. The darkness lasted three hours. At three o'clock, Jesus groaned out of the depths, crying loudly, "*Eloi, Eloi, lama sabachthani?*" which means, "My God, my God, why have you abandoned me?"

Some of the bystanders who heard him said, "Listen, he's calling for Elijah." Someone ran off, soaked a sponge in sour wine, put it on a stick, and gave it to him to drink, saying, "Let's see if Elijah comes to take him down."

But Jesus, with a loud cry, gave his last breath.

THINK

- What do you think Jesus meant by his only words in this passage? How do you arrive at that answer?
- Which do you think is more likely: that Jesus only *felt* abandoned by God or that God actually *did* abandon him? Why?
- When, if ever, have you felt abandoned by God? What were

the circumstances?

• Why would God abandon one of his children—or even *seem* to?

PRAY

Lord, come near to me . . .

READ The Real Absence

From *Telling the Truth*, by Frederick Buechner[1]

The absence of God is not just an idea to conjure with, an emptiness for the preacher to try to furnish, like a house, with chair and sofa, heat and light, to make it livable. The absence of God is just that which is not livable. It is the tears that Jesus wept over Lazarus and the sweat he sweated in the garden and the cry he choked out when his own tongue filled his mouth like a gag. The blackness of the preacher's black gown speaks of the anguish of it. The Bible he preaches out of speaks of it. The prophets and the psalms all speak of the one who is not there when he is most needed, not to mention Noah and Abraham, Gideon, Barak, Samson and David, and the rest of them who, if they did not speak of their anguish, carried it around in their hearts and grew whiskers and wore robes and armor and ephods and stovepipe hats to help conceal it even from themselves because, as the author of Hebrews strips them and all of us bare by putting it, "They all died without having received what was promised" (Heb. 11:13), the anguish of that, of having at most and by no means every Sunday of the year, glimpsed it only from afar like a light on the horizon that could have been only moonshine.

The cross that is a symbol of defeat before it is a symbol of victory speaks also of the absence of God, and Jesus speaks of it. He says, "Seeing they do not see and hearing they do not hear" (Matt. 13:13). He says, "Why does this generation seek a sign? Truly I say to you, no sign will be given to this generation" (Matt. 12:39), and on the cross as far as we are told no sign was given to him either, just a sponge soaked in Dago red and a word of cold comfort from the good there who asked to be remembered in his kingly power, asked him who died without the power to raise spit and looked less like a king than like a street accident. He says, "My God, my God, why have you left me holding the bag, holding the world, when I can hardly any longer hold up my own head?" . . .

The world hides God from us, or we hide ourselves from God, or for reasons of his own God hides himself from us, but however you account for it, he is often more conspicuous by his absence than by his presence, and his absence is much of what we labor under and are heavy laden by. Just as sacramental theology speaks of a doctrine of the Real Presence, maybe it should speak also of a doctrine of the Real Absence because absence can be sacramental, too, a door left open, a chamber of the heart kept ready and waiting.

THINK

- In regards to "the cross that is a symbol of defeat before it is a symbol of victory," do you feel that such "dark times" in the Bible have been given insufficient attention? Why or why not?
- When was the last time a profound defeat in your life eventually became a profound victory?
- What do you think about Buechner's statement that "the prophets and the psalms all speak of the one who is not there when he is most needed"?
- Consider the following: "If God seems silent, it's because *you* interrupted or damaged your connection with God. Don't blame him. Deal with your sin or inattention first, then your connection with God will be restored." How would you respond?

THINK (CONTINUED)

PRAY

Father, lead me out of hiding . . .

READ Is God Out to Lunch?

Psalm 73:11-24

What's going on here? Is God out to lunch?
    Nobody's tending the store.
The wicked get by with everything;
    they have it made, piling up riches.
I've been stupid to play by the rules;
    what has it gotten me?
A long run of bad luck, that's what—
    a slap in the face every time I walk out the door.

If I'd have given in and talked like this,
    I would have betrayed your dear children.
Still, when I tried to figure it out,
    all I got was a splitting headache . . .
Until I entered the sanctuary of God.
    Then I saw the whole picture:
The slippery road you've put them on,
    with a final crash in a ditch of delusions.
In the blink of an eye, disaster!
    A blind curve in the dark, and—nightmare!
We wake up and rub our eyes. . . . Nothing.
    There's nothing to them. And there never was.

When I was beleaguered and bitter,
    totally consumed by envy,
I was totally ignorant, a dumb ox
    in your very presence.
I'm still in your presence,
    but you've taken my hand.
You wisely and tenderly lead me,
    and then you bless me.

THINK

- "The wicked get by with everything." How many times have you thought this? What is the psalmist's own answer to this gripe?
- When was the last time you gave yourself "a splitting headache" trying to figure out where God was when you needed him so badly? What were the circumstances?
- Did you eventually see "the whole picture" in your difficult situation? If so, what opened your eyes?
- Have you spent most of your life hearing God's voice, or have you spent most of your life frustrated by the apparent silence of God? Explain.

PRAY

God, help me to hear . . .

READ   No White Knight

Richard Hendrix (in *Leadership Journal*)[2]

> Second only to suffering, waiting may be the greatest teacher and trainer in godliness, maturity, and genuine spirituality most of us ever encounter.

Nancy Mairs (in *The Sun*)[3]

> God is no white knight who charges into the world to pluck us like distressed damsels from the jaws of dragons or disease. God chooses to become present to and through us. It is up to us to rescue one another.

THINK

- With your temperament, is it easy for you to wait, or is waiting nearly as bad as outright suffering? What are some examples of this in your life?
- Recall a season in your life when waiting proved to be a great "teacher and trainer in godliness, maturity, and genuine spirituality." Think about this.
- Are we wrong to call God *Savior* if he does not "pluck us" from danger, disease, and disaster? If you believe that such claims should be qualified or nuanced, what would you adjust?
- How might your behavior, habits, or perceptions change if suddenly you started believing that God is present to you through other people?

THINK (CONTINUED)

PRAY

Lord, be present to me . . .

READ Silence You Can Cut with a Knife

Matthew 26:36-40,42

Then Jesus went with them to a garden called Gethsemane and
told his disciples, "Stay here while I go over there and pray."
Taking along Peter and the two sons of Zebedee, he plunged
into an agonizing sorrow. Then he said, "This sorrow is crushing
my life out. Stay here and keep vigil with me."

Going a little ahead, he fell on his face, praying, "My Father,
if there is any way, get me out of this. But please, not what I
want. You, what do *you* want?"

When he came back to his disciples, he found them sound
asleep. He said to Peter, "Can't you stick it out with me a single
hour?" . . .

He then left them a second time. Again he prayed, "My
Father, if there is no other way than this, drinking this cup to the
dregs, I'm ready. Do it your way."

From *Abba's Child*, by Brennan Manning[4]

During a writing session early one morning, for no apparent
reason, a pervasive sense of gloom settled in my soul. I stopped
writing and sat down to read the early chapters of the manu-
script. I got so discouraged I considered abandoning the whole
project. I left the house to get the brake tag on the car renewed.
The office was closed. I decided I needed exercise. After jog-
ging two miles on the levee, a thunderstorm hurled sheets of
rain and a howling wind almost blew me into the Mississippi
River. I sat down in the tall grass, vaguely aware of clinging to a
nail-scarred hand. I returned to the office cold and soaked, only
to get a phone call from Roslyn that led to conflict. My feelings
were running rampant—frustration, anger, resentment, fear, self-
pity, depression. I repeated to myself, "I am not my feelings." No
relief. I tried, "This too shall pass." It didn't.

At six that night, emotionally drained and physically spent, I plopped down in a soft chair. I began to pray the Jesus prayer, "Lord Jesus Christ, have mercy on me, a sinner," seeking out His life-giving Spirit. Slowly but perceptibly I awakened to His sacred presence. The loneliness continued but grew gentle, the sadness endured but felt light. Anger and resentment vanished

A hard day, yes. Rattled and unglued, yes. Unable to cope, no. . . .

A single phone call may abruptly alter the tranquil rhythm of our lives. "Your wife was in a serious accident on the Beltway. She is in critical condition at the hospital intensive care unit." Or "I hate to be the bearer of bad news but your son has been arrested for peddling crack cocaine." Or "Your three-year-old daughter was playing with mine by the side of the pool. I left them alone for just a minute, and your daughter . . ."

When tragedy makes its unwelcome appearance and we are deaf to everything but the shriek of our own agony, when courage flies out the window and the world seems to be a hostile, menacing place, it is the hour of our own Gethsemane. No word, however sincere, offers any comfort or consolation. The night is bad. Our minds are numb, our hearts vacant, our nerves shattered. How will we make it through the night? The God of our lonely journey is silent.

THINK

- When in your experience did the peace of Christ settle on you (without rescuing you from your situation) when you really needed it?
- Is it relevant to talk about prayer and results in the same breath, as though answered prayer is a transaction? Or is it just that, a transaction (you say a prayer, and God responds with an answer)?
- Do you believe a lonely Jesus prayed to a silent Father in Gethsemane, as Manning implies? Why or why not?
- Why do you pray? What do you expect from doing it?

THINK (CONTINUED)

PRAY

God, help me to pray . . .

READ I'm Outta Here

"The Collar," by George Herbert

I struck the board, and cried, No more.
I will abroad.
What? shall I ever sigh and pine?
My lines and life are free; free as the road,
Loose as the wind, as large as store.
Shall I be still in suit?
Have I no harvest but a thorn
To let me blood, and not restore
What I have lost with cordiall fruit?
Sure there was wine
Before my sighs did dry it: there was corn
Before my tears did drown it.
Is the year only lost to me?
Have I no bays to crown it?
No flowers, no garlands gay? all blasted?
All wasted?
Not so, my heart: but there is fruit,
And thou hast hands.
Recover all thy sigh-blown age
On double pleasures: leave thy cold dispute
Of what is fit, and not; forsake thy cage,
Thy rope of sands,
Which petty thoughts have made, and made to thee
Good cable, to enforce and draw,
And be thy law,
While thou didst wink and wouldst not see.
Away; take heed:
I will abroad.
Call in thy death's head there: tie up thy fears.
He that forbears
To suit and serve his need,
Deserves his load.

> But as I raved and grew more fierce and wild
> At every word,
> Me thoughts I heard one calling, *Child*:
> And I replied, *My Lord*.

THINK

- Think about the spiritual and emotional states of the poem's narrator. How are these like or unlike your spiritual and emotional states when seeking God?
- What peevish road do you go down when you've had it "up to here" with knocking yourself out for God and getting "nothing" in return?
- What finally stopped the narrator's rant?
- What here resonates with you?

PRAY

God, make yourself known . . .

LIVE

What I Want to Discuss

What have you discovered this week that you definitely want to discuss with your small group? Write that here. Then begin your small-group discussion with these thoughts.

So What?

Use the following space to summarize what you've discovered about the apparent silence of God in your life. Review your "Beginning Place" if you need to remember where you began. How does God's truth impact the "next step" in your journey?

Then What?

What is one practical thing you can do to apply what you've discovered? Describe how you would put this into practice. What steps would you take? Remember to think realistically—an admirable but unreachable goal is as good as no goal. Discuss your goal in your small group to further define it.

How?

Identify how you will be held accountable to the goal you described. Who will be on your support team? What are their responsibilities? How will you measure the success of your plan? Write the details here.

HOW DO I GET MY SPIRITUAL LIFE OUT OF FIRST GEAR?

"All these victory stories I hear from Christians are beginning to get to me. What am I doing wrong?"

A REMINDER:

Before you dive into this study, spend a little time reviewing what you wrote in the previous lesson's "Live" sections. How are you doing? Check with your small-group members and review your progress toward the specified goals. If necessary, adjust your goals and plans, and then recommit to them.

THE BEGINNING PLACE

Listening to many Christian leaders, you could easily conclude that if you don't have a life defined by on-fire, 110 percent, totally sold-out discipleship, there's something wrong with you. You're hot or not. Jesus said as much to the slacker Laodicean Christians: "You're not cold, you're not hot—far better to be either cold or hot! You're stale. You're stagnant. You make me want to vomit" (Revelation 3:15-16). Ouch. No one wants to make the Almighty nauseous.

That may explain the long line of Christians willing to volunteer their white-hot testimonies of God's amazing work in and through them. In a good mood, you're happy for them. When you're feeling rough around the edges, though, their answered prayers and disasters-turned-to-victories and happy tales of having children who all "walk with the Lord"—well, they bother you. They dig at your spiritual confidence. You begin wondering what's wrong with you—why it is that you can go through the same motions as these spiritual superheroes, repeat the same biblical mantras, try to work up the same zeal yet end up with nothing.

Granted, it's tricky. The very existence of so many Protestant denominations illustrates that Christians are working their unique spins to get God's attention, to crawl out of a spiritual ennui, to be successful or fruitful or biblical or pure. The Bible itself seems to offer a dizzying assortment of remedies for your spiritual ailments. Some verses tell you to let go; other verses tell you to hang on. Get out there and be a Christian among pagans; withdraw from those pagans. Don't trust yourself; trust the Christ who is in you. Stop trying so hard; try harder.

No wonder spirituality can be so slippery.

Where or when did you bog down? Where are your wheels spinning and unable to grab traction? Is it all making you feel discouraged or angry?

Use the space below to summarize your beginning place for this lesson. Describe the spiritual plateau you feel stranded on (if you do), what you've tried to do to get off it and start climbing again, and what seems to work for other Christians but not for you. We'll start here and then go deeper.

READ Everything's Fine . . . Right?

Job 19:7

> Look at me—I shout "Murder!" and I'm ignored;
>   I call for help and no one bothers to stop.

From *Your Money or Your Life*, by John Alexander[1]

You'd think we'd do something. I would understand pouring blood at the Pentagon. I would understand quitting one's job and joining a convent to devote one's life to prayer. I would understand trying to get the president of the United States committed to an insane asylum. I would certainly understand retiring to the woods. I would even understand throwing bombs (though I wouldn't accept it). But I do not understand carrying on—selling ice boxes on the burning deck. You'd think people would find some way to say no to hell, some way to say yes to life. But we don't even seem to notice that everything is wrong.

THINK

- When was the last time you looked around and, noticing the calm demeanors of those around you, wondered if you were the only person feeling outrage?
- Why do you think the spiritual doldrums are so resistant? Why is it that, more often than not, it takes a crisis to shake them off?
- In what little, everyday ways do you say "yes" to hell and "no" to life?
- And in what seemingly small ways do you say "no" to hell and "yes" to life?
- What's the least it would take to jar you out of your spiritual lethargy?

THINK

PRAY

God, lead me out of the wilderness . . .

READ For Just Ten Minutes

From *Inside Out*, by Larry Crabb[2]

A good friend of mine recently sat in my office thinking out loud about whatever came to mind. The topics ranged from his marriage (which had its share of disappointments), to his future plans for ministry, to the quality of his walk with the Lord. As the conversation continued his mood became increasingly thoughtful—not gloomy, but quietly and deeply reflective, the kind of mood no one ever feels in a fast-food restaurant.

My friend, I should point out, is a committed Christian, a gifted counselor, and an unusually clear thinker. His life has known a few trials, but nothing remarkably different from what most middle-aged men have experienced. His friends describe him as friendly, hardworking, loyal, and sincere. A few see his spontaneous fun-loving side. Everyone agrees he's a solid, well-adjusted Christian.

After nearly an hour of reflective rambling, his thoughtful mood shifted into a profoundly sad, almost desperate, loneliness. As though talking to no one in particular, he quietly said, "I wonder what it would be like to feel really good for just ten minutes."

THINK

- Was this man spiritually mature? Immature? Fooling himself about his maturity? Godly? Too hard on himself?
- What of this man's loneliness do you know only too well? Do you know what it is like to feel really good for ten minutes?
- What does a maturing Christian man look like on the inside? Does he feel a consistent desire to do what's right? Or does he fight a persistent inner battle between his urges to do wrong and his commitments to do right?
- Do you delight to do God's will, or do you carry a deepened sense of loneliness and struggle? Explain.

- Do you believe that most Christians are happy, or do you suspect that they are pretending, at least to some degree?

PRAY

God, show me what it takes to feel good . . .

READ You're a Failure, So Stop Trying

From *Christ the Tiger*, by Thomas Howard[3]

One [campus] group that attracted me was English in its ori-
gin and had as its specialty something called "the victorious
life." . . . I liked the atmosphere that surrounded this kind of
thinking. These people were not inclined to displays of religious
zeal and enthusiasm, but I felt that they had a deep taproot con-
necting them with spiritual realities that gave them their stead-
fastness and tranquility. In order to have this victorious life one
had to "let go and let God." It was the simplest formula in the
world. Do not try to do for yourself what Christ had already
done for you. You are a failure. You cannot help but sin. But
what do you suppose the Resurrection was all about? Christ rose
a victor over sin as well as death, and now He lives *in* you. The
entire power of the Resurrection is at your disposal. Stop trying
to fight Satan and yourself with your silly little weapons. Go to
the Victor. Christus Victor.

My own problem here was that, after years of attempting
to let go, and repeated attempts to hunch myself over the fence
into the green pasture, or even to let Christ get me over, I could
not get there. I followed meticulously all the steps. I tried, and I
tried not trying. I did everything the speakers told me to do and
not to do. I finally concluded that I was not a candidate for the
victorious life. Cupidity and my own consciousness had a way of
staying alive, although I wanted desperately to believe that I had
been crucified and risen with Christ.

THINK

- Does "the victorious life" sound familiar to you? What is your
  experience with this understanding of Christianity?
- In what aspect of your faith have you white-knuckled yourself
  into trying to do what you believed God wanted you to do yet
  nothing worked?

- When you hear someone speak about a victorious Christian life, what is your immediate and gut reaction (admiration, envy, suspicion, incredulity)? Why?
- What does living a "victorious life" look like in light of the fact that our consciousness and will and struggles don't disappear once we become Christians?

PRAY

Lord, direct me to the truth . . .

READ Fresh Strength for Dropouts

Isaiah 30:15; 40:28-31

GOD, the Master, The Holy of Israel,
>   has this solemn counsel:
"Your salvation requires you to turn back to me
>   and stop your silly efforts to save yourselves.
Your strength will come from settling down
>   in complete dependence on me—
The very thing
>   you've been unwilling to do." . . .

Don't you know anything? Haven't you been listening?
GOD doesn't come and go. God *lasts*.
>   He's Creator of all you can see or imagine.
He doesn't get tired out, doesn't pause to catch his breath.
>   And he knows *everything*, inside and out.
He energizes those who get tired,
>   gives fresh strength to dropouts.
For even young people tire and drop out,
>   young folk in their prime stumble and fall.
But those who wait upon GOD get fresh strength.
>   They spread their wings and soar like eagles,
They run and don't get tired,
>   they walk and don't lag behind.

THINK

- List things that, according to Isaiah, God can do for you.
- List things that Isaiah wrote you can do for yourself.
- Which items in that second list have you done or tried recently? What were the results of those actions?
- Describe what it means to you to "wait upon God." How easy or difficult is that for you?

THINK

PRAY

God, show me how to wait upon you . . .

READ Stuck in Your Ways and Hard to Change

From *The Cloister Walk*, by Kathleen Norris[4]

For years I hated weddings. I used to think it was simply
a cultural prejudice against a ceremony that seemed only
to celebrate sentiment and money, the barbaric custom of
"giving away" a woman, as if she were not a person but prop-
erty. But it ran much deeper, a fear of giving myself to anyone.
And then, one night, when my husband had hidden himself
away and was found by a gentle policeman (who later told
me, "Ma'am, your husband was so *depressed*; I never saw a
man so depressed as that"), I read myself to sleep with the
Song of Songs and found us there, the beloved knocking,
calling, "Open to me, my sister, my love," and my own delayed
response, the selfish thought, in the face of love—"I had put
off my garment, how could I put it on again? I had bathed
my feet; how could I soil them?" The comic scurrying, my bad
timing: "I opened to my beloved, but my beloved had turned
and was gone."

That night I discovered, in the "Song," a religious dimen-
sion to something I'd never fully understood. "When I found
him whom my soul loves, I held him and would not let him go,
until I brought him to my mother's house, into the chamber of
her that conceived me." I had, in fact, brought my husband from
New York City to my grandmother's house in South Dakota, the
house where my mother was born, and now I wondered if this
had been an attempt to build a marriage, to free us from the
distractions of the city so that we could get to know each other.
Maybe love needs space around it, and time. Is love fostered by
time as much as it needs and fosters intimacy?

Yes, I am married, but do I know how to love? Has my
heart been shut for so long? I look up that passage in Paul.
"The two will become one flesh," he says, but only after sput-
tering on for a good long while, trying to make explicit the
comparison between marriage and Christ's love for the church.

Finally, he gives up; I hear exasperation as well as wonder in his voice when he says, "This is a great mystery."

Jeremiah 13:15

Listen. Listen carefully: Don't stay stuck in your ways!
     It's GOD's Message we're dealing with here.

THINK

- Whether married or single, your first love as a Christian is Christ. How have you kept this prime relationship not merely safe but maybe too safe?
- It's hard to change old ways—especially old ways that seem safe. What new, perilous ways do you feel that God may be inviting you to?
- If God showed up in your kitchen tomorrow morning as you shuffled in for your first cup of coffee, what do you imagine he would ask you to do?
- What is "a great mystery" between you and God? Are you content with living with that mystery, or do you need a hard answer or two first?

THINK (CONTINUED)

PRAY

God, speak to me out of the mystery . . .

READ Climb Out of Your Coffins!

Ephesians 5:6-14

Don't let yourselves get taken in by religious smooth talk. God gets furious with people who are full of religious sales talk but want nothing to do with him. Don't even hang around people like that.

You groped your way through that murk once, but no longer. You're out in the open now. The bright light of Christ makes your way plain. So no more stumbling around. Get on with it! The good, the right, the true—these are the actions appropriate for daylight hours. Figure out what will please Christ, and then do it.

Don't waste your time on useless work, mere busywork, the barren pursuits of darkness. Expose these things for the sham they are. It's a scandal when people waste their lives on things they must do in the darkness where no one will see. Rip the cover off those frauds and see how attractive they look in the light of Christ.

> Wake up from your sleep,
> Climb out of your coffins;
> Christ will show you the light!

THINK

- What advice or facts does the apostle have for those groping their way through the murk of religious sales talk?
- List the imperatives Paul lays on his readers.
- Despite the murk you may nonetheless feel yourself in, what is one thing that the bright light of Christ may be illuminating for you right now? How can you get on with that?
- In what ways are you currently trying to figure out what will please Christ? How's it going? What if anything are you learning?

tithes and taxes? Wife swapping wouldn't be too far behind.

There are lots of reasons why spiritual leaders want to hide their inadequacies: because those inadequacies are outright sins and they fear being discovered as sinners or undisciplined Christians or simply weak; because their inadequacies aren't sins but uncertainties, which may seem fatal to acknowledge since they spend so much of their public time dispensing certainties, answers, and solutions; because they really believe that being a godly leader is keeping your doubts private, your weaknesses secret, and your failures under wraps.

Where are you in all this? If you're in a traditional role of spiritual leadership (small-group leader, teacher, elder, deacon) or are simply trying to figure out how to be a spiritual leader at home, what struggles make you feel like a hypocrite? Is it belief or behavior you feel you can't acknowledge to those you lead? What price do you pay by *not* acknowledging it?

Use the space below to summarize your beginning place for this lesson. Describe what you perceive to be your spiritual inadequacies and how forthright about them you are or aren't with the people you lead. Try to put into words how your perceived inadequacies affect you when you're in front of your audience—whether in a church building or under your own roof—and when you're alone with yourself. We'll start here and then go deeper.

THINK (CONTINUED)

PRAY

Lord, help me see your light . . .

LIVE

What I Want to Discuss

What have you discovered this week that you definitely want to discuss with your small group? Write that here. Then begin your small-group discussion with these thoughts.

So What?

Use the following space to summarize what you've discovered about your spiritual inertia, along with any hopes or ways to get your faith in gear again. Review your "Beginning Place" if you need to remember where you began. How does God's truth impact the "next step" in your journey?

Then What?

What is one practical thing you can do to apply what you've discovered? Describe how you would put this into practice. What steps would you take? Remember to think realistically—an admirable but unreachable goal is as good as no goal. Discuss your goal in your small group to further define it.

How?

Identify how you will be held accountable to the goal you described. Who will be on your support team? What are their responsibilities? How will you measure the success of your plan? Write the details here.

I'M SUPPOSED TO LEAD?

"How can I be a spiritual leader when actually I don't know which way is up?"

A REMINDER:

Before you dive into this study, spend a little time reviewing what you wrote in th previous lesson's "Live" sections. How are you doing? Check with your small-gro members and review your progress toward the specified goals. If necessary, ad your goals and plans, and then recommit to them.

THE BEGINNING PLACE

"Well, *someone's* got to be an example around here," said the lor pastor.

He did not speak out of frustration with the immoralit congregation; to the contrary, his church was a model of priate behavior. Rather, the nearly retired minister spoke w of having battened down the personal hatches decades white-knuckling his way through a life of being a paid e existence in a fishbowl. He spoke as if had he cracked o (even for a second) on whatever doubts, anxieties, disap failures, and vices were within him and let his congregati was *really* simmering inside of him, his church would lo in him and, by extension, in his God. *Then* what wou ioners do but throw themselves into alcoholism and ch

READ So You Want to Be a Leader?

1 Timothy 3:1-7

If anyone wants to provide leadership in the church, good! But
there are preconditions: A leader must be well-thought-of, committed to his wife, cool and collected, accessible, and hospitable.
He must know what he's talking about, not be overfond of wine,
not pushy but gentle, not thin-skinned, not money-hungry. He
must handle his own affairs well, attentive to his own children
and having their respect. For if someone is unable to handle his
own affairs, how can he take care of God's church? He must not
be a new believer, lest the position go to his head and the Devil
trip him up. Outsiders must think well of him, or else the Devil
will figure out a way to lure him into his trap.

Titus 1:5-9

Appoint leaders in every town according to my instructions. As
you select them, ask, "Is this man well-thought-of? Are his children believers? Do they respect him and stay out of trouble?"
It's important that a church leader, responsible for the affairs in
God's house, be looked up to—not pushy, not short-tempered,
not a drunk, not a bully, not money-hungry. He must welcome
people, be helpful, wise, fair, reverent, have a good grip on himself, and have a good grip on the Message, knowing how to use
the truth to either spur people on in knowledge or stop them in
their tracks if they oppose it.

THINK

- Have you ever measured yourself against Paul's criteria in these
  two passages? How did you stack up?
- Which of the apostle's criteria, in your opinion, get the most
  public attention? Which get the least? What do you think about
  that?

- How would you respond to someone who said, "Face it— *no one* lives up to this list of qualifications. St. Paul was drafting the *ideal*, not the real"?
- What implications do these passages have for men who feel led to be spiritual leaders at home?

PRAY

Lord, show me how to lead . . .

READ Snapshot of an Ancient Life

Deuteronomy 17:14-17

When you enter the land that GOD, your God, is giving you and take it over and settle down, and then say, "I'm going to get me a king, a king like all the nations around me," make sure you get yourself a king whom GOD, your God, chooses. . . . And make sure he doesn't build up a war machine, amassing military horses and chariots. . . . And make sure he doesn't build up a harem, collecting wives who will divert him from the straight and narrow. And make sure he doesn't pile up a lot of silver and gold.

1 Chronicles 3:1-9

These are the sons that David had while he lived at Hebron: His firstborn was Amnon by Ahinoam of Jezreel;

second, Daniel by Abigail of Carmel;

third, Absalom born of Maacah, daughter of Talmai king of Geshur;

fourth, Adonijah born of Haggith;

fifth, Shephatiah born of Abital;

sixth, Ithream born of his wife Eglah.

He had these six sons while he was in Hebron; he was king there for seven years and six months.

He went on to be king in Jerusalem for another thirty-three years. These are the sons he had in Jerusalem: first Shammua, then Shobab, Nathan, and Solomon. Bathsheba daughter of Ammiel was the mother of these four. And then there were another nine sons: Ibhar, Elishua, Eliphelet, Nogah, Nepheg, Japhia, Elishama, Eliada, Eliphelet—David's sons, plus Tamar their sister. There were other sons by his concubines.

2 Samuel 8:1-4

In the days that followed, David struck hard at the Philistines—
brought them to their knees and took control of the countryside.

He also fought and defeated Moab. He chose two-thirds of
them randomly and executed them. The other third he spared.
So the Moabites fell under David's rule and were forced to bring
tribute.

On his way to restore his sovereignty at the River Euphrates,
David next defeated Hadadezer son of Rehob the king of Zobah.
He captured from him a thousand chariots, seven thousand cav-
alry, and twenty thousand infantry. He hamstrung all the chariot
horses, but saved back a hundred.

2 Samuel 11:2-5,14-15,26-27; 12:1

One late afternoon, David got up from taking his nap and was
strolling on the roof of the palace. From his vantage point on
the roof he saw a woman bathing. The woman was stunningly
beautiful. David sent to ask about her, and was told, "Isn't this
Bathsheba, daughter of Eliam and wife of Uriah the Hittite?"
David sent his agents to get her. After she arrived, he went to
bed with her. (This occurred during the time of "purification" following her period.) Then she returned home. Before long she
realized she was pregnant.

Later she sent word to David: "I'm pregnant." . . .

In the morning David wrote a letter to Joab and sent it
with Uriah. In the letter he wrote, "Put Uriah in the front lines
where the fighting is the fiercest. Then pull back and leave him
exposed so that he's sure to be killed." . . .

When Uriah's wife heard that her husband was dead, she
grieved for her husband. When the time of mourning was over,
David sent someone to bring her to his house. She became his
wife and bore him a son.

But GOD was not at all pleased with what David had done.

1 Chronicles 22:6-8

Then [David] called in Solomon his son and commanded him to build a sanctuary for the GOD of Israel.

David said to Solomon, "I wanted in the worst way to build a sanctuary to honor my GOD. But GOD prevented me, saying, 'You've killed too many people, fought too many wars. You are not the one to honor me by building a sanctuary—you've been responsible for too much killing, too much bloodshed.'"

Acts 13:21-23

After Saul had ruled forty years, God removed him from office and put King David in his place, with this commendation: "I've searched the land and found this David, son of Jesse. He's a man whose heart beats to my heart, a man who will do what I tell him."

From out of David's descendants God produced a Savior for Israel, Jesus, exactly as he promised.

THINK

- What were the three prohibitions God stipulated for Israel's king, when he came along? How did King David measure up to these criteria?
- According to Paul's criteria in 1 Timothy 3 (see previous "Read" section), would King David make an acceptable church leader? Why or why not?
- What does David's story tell you about what it takes to be a spiritual leader?
- After seeing David's, um, "interesting" life choices, are you encouraged or peeved that God called David a man "whose heart beats to my heart"?

THINK (CONTINUED)

PRAY

God, cause my heart to beat as yours . . .

READ So You, Uh, Have Problems, Too?

From *The Preaching Event*, by John Claypool[1]

It began with a telephone call from a Presbyterian minister in
Louisville. He was in real personal anguish, he said, and he
asked the question: "Where does a pastor go for pastoral care?
We are so busy helping other people. Where do we turn when
our needs become overwhelming?

"At any rate," he continued, "I am calling five of you whom
I trust with this request. Would you agree to meet with me in
my study once a week for six times? The only contract will be
that we will try to be honest and hear each other. Perhaps we
can develop enough trust so that we can take off our masks
and show each other where we really hurt. And maybe we
can become a band of brothers who can bequeath healing and
encouragement to each other. I do not know if this will work,
but if it does not, I'll go under for sure!"

I was frankly startled when that conversation was over,
because I had only known this man from a distance, and he
appeared to be "so together" that I would never have dreamed
in a thousand years that he was struggling as he indicated. Then,
too, I had a sense of foreboding about the group he proposed.
I was not at all sure that I could stay in the role of the helper in
that kind of context. I had the fear that I might step over the line
and take off my mask and let some of these wounds that I had
just discovered become visible. And to be honest, the group he
mentioned were ministers with whom I felt a great deal of com-
petition. I wanted them to see me as a winner, not as the person
I was slowly discovering myself to be. Therefore, it was not at all
easy for me to decide what to do. But I suppose if one is hurting
badly enough, he or she will almost do anything.

So the next morning I went to that man's study and touched
for the first time in my life an experience of genuine *koinonia*.
I was absolutely astonished by what began to unfold before my
eyes. For one thing, I discovered that every one of us around

that table was struggling with much the same problems. . . . I
had no idea that behind the façade of successful clergymen were
some of the very same struggles that I was experiencing. We
were all so much more alike than I had realized.

And so one morning, with all the courage that I could muster, I did something that I had never done before. I took off my
mask. I related the story . . . about that old and deep sense of
nobodiness, about how hard I had tried to make a name for
myself and how weary and lonely and frustrated I had become.
I did not realize myself how much pain there was inside until
I began to share it and it gushed forth like the pus in a boil
that at last has been lanced. When I had pretty much emptied
myself, the man in the group for whom I felt the least natural
affinity—an Episcopal rector who was well-born and had all the
graces of Bluegrass aristocracy—was the first to speak.

"I hear you, John," he said, "I hear you. And I know exactly
what you are talking about, because I am walking that road
myself. . . . We need to hear the gospel down in our guts. In the
Sermon on the Mount, Jesus says, 'Ye are the light of the world.'
He does not say, 'You have got to be number one in order to get
light,' or, 'You must out-achieve everybody else in order to earn
light.' He says simply, 'You are light.'" . . .

For the first time in my life, *I felt a sense of grace.* . . . It
also dawned on me that the secret of life is not getting something outside inside by achieving and competing. It is, rather,
getting what is already inside outside by acceptance and self-
giving. . . . I began to taste what the Genesis account suggests
was God's feeling for what he had created—namely, delight,
that childlike wonder that looks at what it has made and says
ecstatically, "It is good, good, very, very good." I began to learn
that things do not have to be perfect to be good, and compared
with never having been at all, whatever one has been dealt in
the act of creation is worthy of celebration.

THINK

- Ever had an experience like Claypool's of "genuine *koinonia*"? What was it like?
- Is among other spiritual leaders the best time and place for a spiritual leader to confess his humanity and fallability?
- What would it look like for a leader to confess these things to those people he leads? How might that impact his ability to lead?
- When was the last time you confessed to someone a feeling or thought or behavior that you felt disqualified you from being *anybody's* spiritual leader? What was the result of that confession?

PRAY

Lord, help me to confess . . .

READ Full of Himself

Romans 7:14-25; 8:1-2

I'm full of myself—after all, I've spent a long time in sin's prison. What I don't understand about myself is that I decide one way, but then I act another, doing things I absolutely despise. So if I can't be trusted to figure out what is best for myself and then do it, it becomes obvious that God's command is necessary.

But I need something *more*! For if I know the law but still can't keep it, and if the power of sin within me keeps sabotaging my best intentions, I obviously need help! I realize that I don't have what it takes. I can will it, but I can't *do* it. I decide to do good, but I don't *really* do it; I decide not to do bad, but then I do it anyway. My decisions, such as they are, don't result in actions. Something has gone wrong deep within me and gets the better of me every time.

It happens so regularly that it's predictable. The moment I decide to do good, sin is there to trip me up. I truly delight in God's commands, but it's pretty obvious that not all of me joins in that delight. Parts of me covertly rebel, and just when I least expect it, they take charge.

I've tried everything and nothing helps. I'm at the end of my rope. Is there no one who can do anything for me? Isn't that the real question?

The answer, thank God, is that Jesus Christ can and does. He acted to set things right in this life of contradictions where I want to serve God with all my heart and mind, but am pulled by the influence of sin to do something totally different.

With the arrival of Jesus, the Messiah, that fateful dilemma is resolved. Those who enter into Christ's being-here-for-us no longer have to live under a continuous, low-lying black cloud. A new power is in operation. The Spirit of life in Christ, like a strong wind, has magnificently cleared the air, freeing you from a fated lifetime of brutal tyranny at the hands of sin and death.

THINK

- "I can will it, but I can't *do* it." Ever feel like that as a spiritual leader? You mean well yet you just can't *do* what you want to do, at least as consistently? To what degree does this describe you?
- When in your life as a leader did you feel lowest about this sort of thing?
- When in your life as a leader did you feel most successful at this?
- Is guilt part of this mix in you? Why or why not?

PRAY

God, help me to match your will with my actions . . .

READ   Irritable, Vain, and Saintly

From *Unfinished Business*, by Donald Joy[2]

> Within a few years, when I interrupted him at his pastoral office
> adjacent to a college, I found the waiting room nicely populated
> with people waiting their turn for appointments. You might
> guess what they come to talk about. I warned Mel that when he
> had passed through the dark days of dealing with his compulsive
> masturbation there would be a sign written on his forehead: Mel
> Can Help You! But it is only legible to those who are passing
> through a dark cloud very like the one he had survived.

**Kathleen Norris in *Great Spirits 1000–2000: The 52 Christians Who Most
Influenced Their Millennium***[3]

> Acknowledging the fact that these "great spirits" were in fact
> ordinary people, irritable, rash, vain, and all too often prone to
> failure, does not diminish them or dilute the divine mystery that
> illuminates their lives.

George Bernard Shaw

> If you cannot get rid of the family skeleton, you may as well
> make it dance.

THINK

- Who do you know whose life is open enough for you to recognize moral failure, great vanity, or some other weakness yet
  is a profound source of spiritual insight and counsel for you?
- Why do you suppose "the dark days" of Bible heroes are not
  the subject of as many sermons and Bible studies as those
  people's virtuous and exemplary sides?
- What may be an unfortunate consequence of showcasing one's
  virtues and de-emphasizing one's faults?

• What skeleton's are in your personal closet? How could you make them dance? Why would you want to make them dance?

PRAY

God, teach me to be honest . . .

READ   A Common Man

From *Abba's Child*, by Brennan Manning[4]

John Eagan, who died in 1987, was an ordinary man. An unheralded high school teacher in Milwaukee, he spent thirty years ministering with youth. He never wrote a book, appeared on television, converted the masses, or gathered a reputation for holiness. He ate, slept, drank, biked cross-country, roamed through the woods, taught classes, and prayed. And he kept a journal, published shortly after his death [*A Traveler Toward the Dawn*, Loyola University Press]. . . .

Eagan, a flawed man with salient weaknesses and character defects, learned that brokenness is proper to the human condition, that we must forgive ourselves for being unlovable, inconsistent, incompetent, irritable, and potbellied, and he knew that his sins could not keep him from God.

THINK

- Is John Eagan an "ordinary man," a "flawed man," a saint? Explain.
- How does Eagan compare with you?
- How comfortable are you with the idea that an "ordinary man" could be saint material? Why?
- How does this support the idea that all believers are saints?

THINK (CONTINUED)

PRAY

God, direct me in my ordinariness . . .

LIVE

What I Want to Discuss

What have you discovered this week that you definitely want to discuss with your small group? Write that here. Then begin your small-group discussion with these thoughts.

So What?

Use the following space to summarize what you've discovered about the sense of spiritual inadequacy you may feel. Review your "Beginning Place" if you need to remember where you began. How does God's truth impact the "next step" in your journey?

Then What?

What is one practical thing you can do to apply what you've discovered? Describe how you would put this into practice. What steps would you take? Remember to think realistically—an admirable but unreachable goal is as good as no goal. Discuss your goal in your small group to further define it.

How?

Identify how you will be held accountable to the goal you described. Who will be on your support team? What are their responsibilities? How will you measure the success of your plan? Write the details here.

I'VE LOST THE MAP FOR MY SPIRITUAL JOURNEY

"Some things I've believed all my life are beginning
to shuffle around—and I don't know how to
deal with these changes."

A REMINDER:

Before you dive into this study, spend a little time reviewing what you wrote in the previous lesson's "Live" sections. How are you doing? Check with your small-group members and review your progress toward the specified goals. If necessary, adjust your goals and plans, and then recommit to them.

THE BEGINNING PLACE

On your spiritual growth journey, you may have encountered some surprises that have led to uncertainty about your beliefs. These surprises may have taken the form of the sold-out-to-doing-things-the-Baptist-way leader of your youth group dropping off the radar, only to be found later a member of the Orthodox Church. Or the adult children of your Methodist friends discovering the high-octane worship of a charismatic church and letting their Methodist parents know that they're praying for them to exchange their dead, formal, ritualistic religion for a fervent and biblical faith.

People around you have always been zigging and zagging in their spiritual journey, but they're not the ones who get the press. The road you hear preached and taught and published and broadcast is usually much more predictable and much less risky than you may have experienced. And when you first notice that you're no longer on the beaten path, you're disinclined to talk about it. Many Christians spend years wondering what's wrong with them—wondering how they got on this two-lane county road while the freeway in the distance continued to carry happy, busy Christians along on the way to their spiritual goals.

If you've felt anything like this, you're in good company. A casual flip through any history of Christianity reveals that Christians who grew differently from the accepted norm were ignored, ridiculed, marginalized—or declared heretics. Arminius, Savonarola, Francis of Assisi, Joan of Arc, John Wesley—the Christian church came down hard on these people because they had the courage or the naïveté to speak aloud of their personal experience with Jesus, and because their experiences contradicted The Norm. "When I gave food to the poor," recalled Brazilian archbishop Dom H. Camara, "they called me a saint. When I asked why the poor were hungry, they called me a communist."

What is spiritual maturity supposed to look like, anyway? Where did you acquire your picture of it? And what price (if any) are you paying for the unanticipated detour you're taking from The Accepted Path, whatever that may be?

Use the space below to summarize your beginning place for this lesson. Describe what your spiritual growth is looking like, especially if its direction or form may be surprising to you. Try to put into words the kinds of questions you have now that five or ten or twenty years ago you never dreamed you'd have. We'll start here and then go deeper.

READ Whiplash or Slow Turning?

From *Graceland*, by Tim McLaughlin[1]

Our ideal of Christian conversion owes most of its imagery to the many tellings of St. Paul's conversion (Acts 9), when he was still Saul of Tarsus, a fiercely zealous Pharisee bent on keeping Judaism pure—the Jerusalem bounty hunter on the road with an arrest warrant in his hand for heretic Christians in Damascus. He was interrupted en route to his mission, however, by the same Jesus whose followers he was out to get. Knocked off his feet and blinded by a flash of light, he immediately knew who it was he was dealing with and became instantly compliant.

Or the jailer in the prisons of Philippi (Acts 16), who within minutes goes from content pagan to desperate searcher to grateful Christian, thanks to a career-threatening earthquake and the providential presence of St. Paul among the prisoners.

"Once I was blind, but now I see," go the lyrics to at least one gospel song. Dark-light, off-on, lost-saved. The spiritual U-turn of conversion is as popularly represented—and often experienced—as a Toyota would make it: a quick one-eighty in an intersection, and two seconds later accelerating in the opposite direction.

Such conversions are visible, measurable, and gratifying. Yet many experience conversion like an ocean-going oil tanker, whose bulk requires miles to turn around. And when you're aboard such vessels as they turn, it is not always obvious that you *are* turning—the ship is huge, and there are few if any points of reference at sea by which to gauge the rate of your turn. Until, that is, the turn is almost completed and you realized by unmistakable signs that you're headed in the opposite direction now. . . .

In many Christians the timetable is all backwards, contrary to the popularized order of love events with God, which goes something like this:

- You ignore God, or actively dislike him.
- You get saved—and your love affair with the Savior begins.

- The early season of salvation is colored by newness, fervor, enthusiasm—in short, the romance of young faith. Spiritual passion spikes early.
- Then comes settling in. The spike of passion that characterized your romantic season levels out into a gradually maturing relationship with God.

Yet the experience of a lot of Christians contradicts this neat, logical order. Some, for example, experience this:

- You can hardly remember *not* being a Christian. It was in the air from your earliest memories, and you can't exactly say when it went from there into your heart.
- Christianity becomes an unconscious framework for how you perceive life. No passion here, just a matter-of-factness with which you interpret your world.
- In adolescence or young adulthood you awaken intellectually to your faith. Bible study, biblical languages, and the idealism of Christian community capture your imagination. A big spike here of love of learning about God, if not of spiritual passion.
- A decade or two or three later your world comes undone, your tightly constructed theories about God unwind and get all tangled up, your battered theologies are reduced to "Jesus loves me, this I know"—and for some reason, that is enough, and you find yourself crying often, and at the drop of a hat, why you're not sure—gratitude is part of it, and loss and yearning, and some of it feels like praying.

Welcome to your season of passion.

THINK

- Trace the stages of *your* spiritual journey.
- What was the nature of your conversion? Passionate? Kicking-and-screaming? Matter-of-fact? Seemingly gradual or even unconscious?
- Have you ever described your conversion to an individual or a group? Why or why not?
- How comfortable or distressed are you with where you are spiritually right now?

PRAY

Father, show me the next turn for my journey . . .

READ Is That a Way to Run an Army?

Judges 6:11-16; 7:1-7,16-23

One day the angel of GOD came and sat down under the oak in Ophrah that belonged to Joash the Abiezrite, whose son Gideon was threshing wheat in the winepress, out of sight of the Midianites. The angel of GOD appeared to him and said,

"GOD is with you,

O mighty warrior!"

Gideon replied, "With *me*, my master? If GOD is with us, why has all this happened to us? Where are all the miracle-wonders our parents and grandparents told us about, telling us, 'Didn't GOD deliver us from Egypt?' The fact is, GOD has nothing to do with us—he has turned us over to Midian."

But GOD faced him directly: "Go in this strength that is yours. Save Israel from Midian. Haven't I just sent you?"

Gideon said to him, "*Me*, my master? How and with what could I ever save Israel? Look at me. My clan's the weakest in Manasseh and I'm the runt of the litter."

GOD said to him, "I'll be with you. Believe me, you'll defeat Midian as one man." . . .

Jerub-Baal (Gideon) got up early the next morning, all his troops right there with him. They set up camp at Harod's Spring. The camp of Midian was in the plain, north of them near the Hill of Moreh.

GOD said to Gideon, "You have too large an army with you. I can't turn Midian over to them like this—they'll take all the credit, saying, 'I did it all myself,' and forget about me. Make a public announcement: 'Anyone afraid, anyone who has any qualms at all, may leave Mount Gilead now and go home.'" Twenty-two companies headed for home. Ten companies were left.

GOD said to Gideon: "There are still too many. Take them down to the stream and I'll make a final cut. When I say, 'This one goes with you,' he'll go. When I say, 'This one doesn't go,' he won't go." So Gideon took the troops down to the stream.

GOD said to Gideon: "Everyone who laps with his tongue, the way a dog laps, set on one side. And everyone who kneels to drink, drinking with his face to the water, set to the other side." Three hundred lapped with their tongues from their cupped hands. All the rest knelt to drink.

GOD said to Gideon: "I'll use the three hundred men who lapped at the stream to save you and give Midian into your hands. All the rest may go home." . . .

He divided the three hundred men into three companies. He gave each man a trumpet and an empty jar, with a torch in the jar. He said, "Watch me and do what I do. When I get to the edge of the camp, do exactly what I do. When I and those with me blow the trumpets, you also, all around the camp, blow your trumpets and shout, 'For GOD and for Gideon!'"

Gideon and his hundred men got to the edge of the camp at the beginning of the middle watch, just after the sentries had been posted. They blew the trumpets, at the same time smashing the jars they carried. All three companies blew the trumpets and broke the jars. They held the torches in their left hands and the trumpets in their right hands, ready to blow, and shouted, "A sword for GOD and for Gideon!" They were stationed all around the camp, each man at his post. The whole Midianite camp jumped to its feet. They yelled and fled. When the three hundred blew the trumpets, GOD aimed each Midianite's sword against his companion, all over the camp. They ran for their lives—to Beth Shittah, toward Zererah, to the border of Abel Meholah near Tabbath.

Israelites rallied from Naphtali, from Asher, and from all over Manasseh. They had Midian on the run.

THINK

- How might you have felt as a member of this army? How is this like the way you feel about your spiritual journey?
- How would you respond to someone who advised you,

"Whatever you think the coming stages of your life will look like, forget it, for God is a God of surprises"?

- What if anything about your spiritual journey so far has been somewhat predictable?
- What if anything about your spiritual journey so far has been wilder than you could have ever imagined?
- How can this Bible story encourage you as you think about the spiritual path you're on?

PRAY

Lord, teach me in the surprises . . .

READ Keep Jesus to Yourself

From *Abounding Faith: A Treasury of Wisdom*, by M. Scott Peck[2]

Fifteen years ago I was involved with a team of people that included a young woman I'll call Mary. Mary was then a vocally "fundamentalist" Christian. She seemed unable to speak more than two sentences in sequence without at least one of them including the reverentially intoned name of Jesus. This caused considerable friction. Because I was at the time something of a mentor to her, Mary came to ask me why she was seemingly alienating the other members of the team.

"It's because of your piety," I explained. "You're so public about it, they feel they're being preached to, and they resent it. They want you as a teammate, not a preacher."

"But what can I do about it?" she inquired in total innocence.

"What you shouldn't do is give up one shred of your faith," I responded. "What you should do is to keep it private. You know," I continued, "I've heard tell of certain Christian monks and nuns who upon occasion practice a strange kind of spiritual discipline. They take a vow—just as they would a vow of poverty or chastity or obedience—to not speak the name of Jesus out loud for a year. They remain free to use his name in their hearts and private prayer, but they renounce their need to speak it publicly. As I said, it's a strange kind of discipline, but I wonder if it wouldn't be a useful one for you at this particular point."

I am unaccustomed to my advice being followed to the letter. But to my amazement, over the year that followed Mary never mentioned Jesus at any team meeting. She rapidly became one of the most successful and constructive team members. After the year she confessed to me she'd not only kept her vow on the team but with all the other friends in her life. "It's bizarre," she said. "Jesus has become ever more important to me over the past year, but I no longer have the slightest need to talk about him."

This has been a mere vignette. But let me say this: I have never seen anyone grow so rapidly, not only in that year but in the years to follow. Indeed, it was not long before Mary had become my mentor and one of the greatest spiritual leaders it has been my privilege to know.

THINK

- What advice would *you* have given Mary?
- If you had been the one receiving Peck's advice, how readily would you have followed it? Why?
- Do you feel that the results of Mary's yearlong silence (becoming an invaluable team member and acquiring a deeper spirituality) were predictable, or were they the result of some mystical change? Explain.
- When in your life have you felt as though you were heading in a fruitless direction, only to discover later that things turned out great after all?

PRAY

God, when I don't understand the path I'm on . . .

READ Two Millennia of Tradition Gone Before Lunch

Acts 10:1-29

There was a man named Cornelius who lived in Caesarea, captain of the Italian Guard stationed there. He was a thoroughly good man. He had led everyone in his house to live worshipfully before God, was always helping people in need, and had the habit of prayer. One day about three o'clock in the afternoon he had a vision. An angel of God, as real as his next-door neighbor, came in and said, "Cornelius."

Cornelius stared hard, wondering if he was seeing things. Then he said, "What do you want, sir?"

The angel said, "Your prayers and neighborly acts have brought you to God's attention. Here's what you are to do. Send men to Joppa to get Simon, the one everyone calls Peter. He is staying with Simon the Tanner, whose house is down by the sea."

As soon as the angel was gone, Cornelius called two servants and one particularly devout soldier from the guard. He went over with them in great detail everything that had just happened, and then sent them off to Joppa.

The next day as the three travelers were approaching the town, Peter went out on the balcony to pray. It was about noon. Peter got hungry and started thinking about lunch. While lunch was being prepared, he fell into a trance. He saw the skies open up. Something that looked like a huge blanket lowered by ropes at its four corners settled on the ground. Every kind of animal and reptile and bird you could think of was on it. Then a voice came: "Go to it, Peter—kill and eat."

Peter said, "Oh, no, Lord. I've never so much as tasted food that was not kosher."

The voice came a second time: "If God says it's okay, it's okay."

This happened three times, and then the blanket was pulled back up into the skies.

As Peter, puzzled, sat there trying to figure out what it all meant, the men sent by Cornelius showed up at Simon's front door. They called in, asking if there was a Simon, also called Peter, staying there. Peter, lost in thought, didn't hear them, so the Spirit whispered to him, "Three men are knocking at the door looking for you. Get down there and go with them. Don't ask any questions. I sent them to get you."

Peter went down and said to the men, "I think I'm the man you're looking for. What's up?"

They said, "Captain Cornelius, a God-fearing man well-known for his fair play—ask any Jew in this part of the country—was commanded by a holy angel to get you and bring you to his house so he could hear what you had to say." Peter invited them in and made them feel at home.

The next morning he got up and went with them. Some of his friends from Joppa went along. A day later they entered Caesarea. Cornelius was expecting them and had his relatives and close friends waiting with him. The minute Peter came through the door, Cornelius was up on his feet greeting him—and then down on his face worshiping him! Peter pulled him up and said, "None of that—I'm a man and only a man, no different from you."

Talking things over, they went on into the house, where Cornelius introduced Peter to everyone who had come. Peter addressed them, "You know, I'm sure that this is highly irregular. Jews just don't do this—visit and relax with people of another race. But God has just shown me that no race is better than any other. So the minute I was sent for, I came, no questions asked. But now I'd like to know why you sent for me."

THINK

- How do you think Peter would have reacted to Cornelius (a Gentile, not a Jew) had he not first had his animals-on-a-blanket trance?

- Have you ever felt that God was trying to convince you of something—but to actually believe it would throw out something you were raised and taught to believe in? Describe this experience.
- What "kosher" areas of your life has God invaded and rearranged?

PRAY

Lord, rearrange my thoughts . . .

READ The Hamster Wheel of Faith

From *Water from Stone*, by M. Wayne Brown[3]

We want to know what's happening to us and why it's happening. As one of my clients said at the beginning of her first session, "I don't even need to know where I'm going; I would consider counseling a great success if I could just get a handle on where I am." . . .

I am . . . convinced that trust in the security of Christian principles is being confused with faith in God. Rather than engage a faith that requires, well, a little too much faith (not to mention the inherent wrestling), we find safe harbor in the surrogate stability of Right Christian Living. To allow God's uncontrollable ways to work their power in our lives is so much more refreshing and inspiring and, yes, less predictable. This is the way of faith, which is the very heart of the Christian's journey.

In the guise of good stewardship and sound thinking, our faith is fashioning for itself a well-oiled hamster wheel. Though secure and productive (it spins well), the contraption leaves little to the imagination. Granted, for the harried traveler nothing is more calming than the hum of a spinning wheel. But nothing is more numbing.

THINK

- Are you on familiar or unfamiliar ground right now in your spiritual experience? Explain.
- When you read Brown's distinction between "Christian principles" and "faith in God," did you agree with these words or react negatively to them? Why?
- What do you think of Brown's opinion of a faith that is predictable, secure, productive, and unimaginative?

THINK (CONTINUED)

PRAY

Father, keep me from becoming numb . . .

READ Regrets

From *With the Huckleberry Christ*, by Kristen Johnson Ingram[4]

> I found him in stages from my infancy through my adulthood; but when I really found him, all in one piece, it was too late for me to go to seminary; my bones ached too much to spend the rest of my life in a convent; and I was too bound by love for my children to run away with God, except within the secret of my heart.

THINK

- How and when (early or later in life) did you find God "all in one piece"?
- Is there anything that happened or didn't happen along your faith journey that you regret? Something that occurred too late or early for you to take advantage of it?
- Ever wonder sometimes that you may have missed a calling? How do you deal with that?
- How does the truth of where you are now in your journey inform how you see spiritual growth for tomorrow?

PRAY

God, help me "run away with" you . . .

LIVE

What I Want to Discuss

What have you discovered this week that you definitely want to discuss with your small group? Write that here. Then begin your small-group discussion with these thoughts.

So What?

Use the following space to summarize what you've discovered about the "differentness" of your spiritual experience at the moment. Review your "Beginning Place" if you need to remember where you began. How does God's truth impact the "next step" in your journey?

Then What?

What is one practical thing you can do to apply what you've discovered? Describe how you would put this into practice. What steps would you take? Remember to think realistically—an admirable but unreachable goal is as good as no goal. Discuss your goal in your small group to further define it.

How?

Identify how you will be held accountable to the goal you described. Who will be on your support team? What are their responsibilities? How will you measure the success of your plan? Write the details here.

HOPE

"Stopping the car to listen for God."

A TIME TO REVIEW

We've come to the final lesson in our *Chasing God with Three Flat Tires* discussion guide, but this is not an ending place. Hopefully, you've been discovering some truths about your life and seen opportunity for change—positive change. But no matter what has brought you to lesson 8, you know that it's only a pause in your journey.

You may have uncovered behaviors or thoughts that demanded change. Perhaps you've already changed them. Will the changes stick? How will you continue to take the momentum from this study into next week, next month, and next year? Use this lesson as a time to not only review what you discovered but also determine how you'll stay on track tomorrow.

Talk about your plans with small-group members, commit your plans to prayer, and then do what you say you'll do. As you move forward with a renewed sense of purpose, you'll become more confident approaching the challenge of growing your faith. And with the confidence will come, gradually, more success at becoming the man you want to become.

READ   Church Leaves Me Cold

Psalm 100:4

> Enter with the password: "Thank you!"
>   Make yourselves at home, talking praise.
>   Thank him. Worship him.

THINK

- What's the distance between this psalmic ideal and your church? Between this psalmic ideal and you?
- Who is worship for—you or God? Who is intended to receive good feelings, warm feelings?

PRAY

God, help me worship . . .

LIVE

- How does God's truth impact the "next step" in your journey?
- How will you get there?
- How will you be held accountable?

READ   What Quiet Time?

Matthew 6:6-9

"Here's what I want you to do: Find a quiet, secluded place so you won't be tempted to role-play before God. Just be there as simply and honestly as you can manage. The focus will shift from you to God, and you will begin to sense his grace.

"The world is full of so-called prayer warriors who are prayer-ignorant. They're full of formulas and programs and advice, peddling techniques for getting what you want from God. Don't fall for that nonsense. This is your Father you are dealing with, and he knows better than you what you need. With a God like this loving you, you can pray very simply."

THINK

- What will you need to do in order not to role-play before God?
- Do formulas and programs and advice about praying help you? If so, what does that say about your prayers?

PRAY

Lord, teach me what a "quiet time" should be . . .

LIVE

- How does God's truth impact the "next step" in your journey?
- How will you get there?
- How will you be held accountable?

READ Stewardship of Fools?

2 Corinthians 9:6-7

Remember: A stingy planter gets a stingy crop; a lavish planter gets a lavish crop. I want each of you to take plenty of time to think it over, and make up your own mind what you will give. That will protect you against sob stories and arm-twisting. God loves it when the giver delights in the giving.

THINK

- How much or what proportion of your weekly or monthly income would you give if you took "plenty of time to think it over"?
- Have you ever delighted in giving? If so, recall the circumstances of that leg of your faith journey.

PRAY

God, remove my uncertainty about money . . .

LIVE

- How does God's truth impact the "next step" in your journey?
- How will you get there?
- How will you be held accountable?

READ So, How Long Will God Be On Vacation?

Psalm 73:11-13

> What's going on here? Is God out to lunch?
>> Nobody's tending the store.
> The wicked get by with everything;
>> they have it made, piling up riches.
> I've been stupid to play by the rules;
>> what has it gotten me?

THINK

- How do you move forward in your faith when you feel that God is "out to lunch"?
- When life hits you below the belt, do you tend to blame God for it? Why or why not?

PRAY

God, show me the truth about you . . .

LIVE

- How does God's truth impact the "next step" in your journey?
- How will you get there?
- How will you be held accountable?

READ How Do I Get My Spiritual Life Out of First Gear?

Ephesians 5:8

> You groped your way through that murk once, but no longer. You're out in the open now. The bright light of Christ makes your way plain. So no more stumbling around. Get on with it!

THINK

- What murk are you in, are you emerging from, or have you finally left behind?
- What's one thing you can "get on with" tomorrow?

PRAY

God, make my way plain . . .

LIVE

- How does God's truth impact the "next step" in your journey?
- How will you get there?
- How will you be held accountable?

READ I'm Supposed to Lead?

Romans 7:14-15

I'm full of myself—after all, I've spent a long time in sin's prison. What I don't understand about myself is that I decide one way, but then I act another, doing things I absolutely despise.

THINK

- In what ways do you have a difficult time acting according to your beliefs?
- What comfort do you find in Paul's admission that it's no easy thing to do what we ought? How does that impact how you see yourself as a leader?

PRAY

Lord, help me to do your will . . .

LIVE

- How does God's truth impact the "next step" in your journey?
- How will you get there?
- How will you be held accountable?

READ I've Lost the Map for My Spiritual Journey

Acts 10:28

> Peter addressed them, "You know, I'm sure that this is highly irregular. Jews just don't do this—visit and relax with people of another race. But God has just shown me that no race is better than any other."

THINK

- Simon Peter was spiritually stretched in this circumstance. In what ways are *you* being spiritually stretched?
- How can friends, family members, leaders, and small-group members help you grow into a new and more spiritually healthy place?

PRAY

God, prepare my heart for change . . .

LIVE

- How does God's truth impact the "next step" in your journey?
- How will you get there?
- How will you be held accountable?

NOTES

LESSON 1

1. Frederick Buechner, *Wishful Thinking: A Seeker's ABC*, revised and expanded (San Francisco: HarperSanFrancisco, 1993), p. 17.
2. Larry Crabb, *Inside Out* (Colorado Springs, Colo.: NavPress, 1988), pp. 84-86.
3. Annie Dillard in *The Sun* (May 2000).
4. Bob Rognlien, *Experiential Worship: Encountering God with Heart, Soul, Mind, and Strength* (Colorado Springs, Colo.: NavPress, 2005), pp. 50 51.

LESSON 2

1. Madeleine L'Engle, *Two-Part Invention: The Story of a Marriage* (New York: Harper & Row, 1988), p. 185.
2. "The Sayings of the Fathers," in *Seeking a Purer Spiritual Life: The Desert Mothers and Fathers*, ed. Keith Beasley-Topliffe (Nashville: The Upper Room, 2000), p. 57.
3. Frederick Buechner, *Wishful Thinking: A Seeker's ABC*, revised and expanded (San Francisco: HarperSanFrancisco, 1993), pp. 9, 12.
4. J. P. Moreland, *Love Your God with All Your Mind: The Role of Reason in the Life of the Soul* (Colorado Springs, Colo.: NavPress, 1997), p. 165.
5. Thomas Moore, *Meditations: On the Monk Who Dwells in Daily Life* (New York: HarperCollins, 1994), p. 83.

LESSON 3

1. Jerry Bridges, *The Discipline of Grace: God's Role and Our Role in the Pursuit of Holiness* (Colorado Springs, Colo.: NavPress, 1994), p. 37.
2. Tertullian, *Apology and De Spectaculis*, XXXIX, in *Selections from Early Christian Writers*, by Henry Melvill Gwatkin (Grand Rapids, Mich.: Revell, n.d.), p. 117.

3. 30 Hour Famine with Tim McLaughlin, *Fed Up: Showing the World You Can Make a Difference* (Nashville: W Publishing, 2004), pp. 19-21.
4. Thomas Moore, *Meditations: On the Monk Who Dwells in Daily Life* (New York: HarperCollins, 1994), p. 79.

LESSON 4
1. Frederick Buechner, *Telling the Truth: The Gospel as Tragedy, Comedy, and Fairy Tale* (San Francisco: HarperSanFrancisco, 1977), pp. 41-43.
2. Richard Hendrix, in *Leadership Journal* (Summer 1986), p. 59.
3. Nancy Mairs in *The Sun* (May 2000).
4. Brennan Manning, *Abba's Child: The Cry of the Heart for Intimate Belonging* (Colorado Springs, Colo.: NavPress, 2002), pp. 104-106.

LESSON 5
1. John Alexander, *Your Money or Your Life: A New Look at Jesus' View of Wealth and Power* (New York: HarperCollins, 1986).
2. Larry Crabb, *Inside Out* (Colorado Springs, Colo.: NavPress, 1988), pp. 30-31.
3. Thomas Howard, *Christ the Tiger* (San Francisco: Ignatius Press, 1967/1990), pp. 36-37.
4. Kathleen Norris, *The Cloister Walk* (New York: Riverhead Books, 1996), pp. 109-110.

LESSON 6
1. John Claypool, *The Preaching Event* (New York: Harper & Row, 1989), pp. 73-77, 79.
2. Donald Joy, *Unfinished Business: How a Man Can Make Peace with His Past* (Colorado Springs, Colo.: Victor, 1989).
3. Kathleen Norris, foreword to *Great Spirits 1000–2000: The Fifty-two Christians Who Most Influenced Their Millennium*, ed. Selina O'Grady and John Wilkins (Mahwah, N.J.: Paulist Press, 2002).
4. Brennan Manning, *Abba's Child: The Cry of the Heart for Intimate Belonging* (Colorado Springs, Colo.: NavPress, 2002), p. 50.

LESSON 7
1. Tim McLaughlin, *Graceland: A Collection of Songs, Discussion Starters, and Bible Studies About the Journey from Lost to Found* (Grand Rapids, Mich.: Zondervan, 2003), pp. 31, 77-78.
2. M. Scott Peck, introduction to *Abounding Faith: A Treasury of Wisdom*, ed. M. Scott Peck (Kansas City: Andrews McMeel Publishing, 2003).
3. M. Wayne Brown, *Water from Stone: When "Right Christian Living" Has Left You Spiritually Dry* (Colorado Springs, Colo.: NavPress, 2004), pp. 97, 103-104.
4. Kristen Johnson Ingram, *With the Huckleberry Christ: A Spiritual Journey* (Minneapolis: Winston Press, 1985).